Praise for Bill Zoellick's *Web Engagement*

"Judging from the inquiries that we, as a supplier of both e-business and CRM software, get from prospects and clients, I think Bill Zoellick has done a masterful job of answering all the important questions. I would love to have copies of this book today to send out to our new e-business customers and to legacy (i.e., client/server) customers to acquaint them with the brave new world of electronic business in the new millennium."

  —Dr. Peter C. Patton, Chief Technologist, Lawson Software

"Bill Zoellick's book serves as a well-thought-out and carefully explained guide to anyone tasked with developing an architecture for web business strategy. It is both an introduction and a valuable reference for anyone building a web business plan."

  —Frank Gilbane, President, Bluebill Advisors, Inc.,
   Editor, *The Gilbane Report*

"I especially liked Bill Zoellick's approach to personalization on the web. This is *the* major future success issue for web page owners. His approach to business models is fine, and he clearly highlights the distinctions between B2C and B2B approaches."

  —Ron Radice, Principal Partner, Software Technology Transition

"Bill Zoellick has done a fine job of explaining the critical process of gathering web user information in order to attain e-business goals. He clearly maps the conditions under which personalization is warranted and illustrates the potential benefits."

  —Kevin Dick, Author of *XML: A Manager's Guide*,
   Founder, Kevin Dick Associates

Web Engagement

Addison-Wesley Information Technology Series
Capers Jones, Series Editor

The information technology (IT) industry is in the public eye now more than ever before because of a number of major issues in which software technology and national policies are closely related. As the use of software expands, there is a continuing need for business and software professionals to stay current with the state of the art in software methodologies and technologies. The goal of the Addison-Wesley Information Technology Series is to cover any and all topics that affect the IT community: These books illustrate and explore how information technology can be aligned with business practices to achieve business goals and support business imperatives. Addison-Wesley has created this innovative series to empower you with the benefits of the industry experts' experience.

For more information point your browser to
http://www.awl.com/cseng/series/it/

Wayne Applehans, Alden Globe, and Greg Laugero, *Managing Knowledge: A Practical Web-Based Approach.* ISBN: 0-201-43315-X

Gregory C. Dennis and James R. Rubin, *Mission-Critical Java™ Project Management: Business Strategies, Applications, and Development.* ISBN: 0-201-32573-X

Kevin Dick, *XML: A Manager's Guide.* ISBN: 0-201-43335-4

Jill Dyché, *e-Data: Turning Data into Information with Data Warehousing.* ISBN: 0-201-65780-5

Capers Jones, *Software Assessments, Benchmarks, and Best Practices.* ISBN: 0-201-48542-7

Capers Jones, *The Year 2000 Software Problem: Quantifying the Costs and Assessing the Consequences.* ISBN: 0-201-30964-5

Ravi Kalakota and Marcia Robinson, *e-Business: Roadmap for Success.* ISBN: 0-201-60480-9

David Linthicum, *Enterprise Application Integration.* ISBN: 0-201-61583-5

Sergio Lozinsky, *Enterprise-Wide Software Solutions: Integration Strategies and Practices.* ISBN: 0-201-30971-8

Patrick O'Beirne, *Managing the Euro in Information Systems: Strategies for Successful Changeover.* ISBN: 0-201-60482-5

Mai-lan Tomsen, *Killer Content: Strategies for Web Content and E-Commerce.* ISBN: 0-201-65786-4

Bill Wiley, *Essential System Requirements: A Practical Guide to Event-Driven Methods.* ISBN: 0-201-61606-8

Bill Zoellick, *Web Engagement: Connecting to Customers in e-Business.* ISBN: 0-201-65766-X

Web Engagement

Connecting to Customers in e-Business

Bill Zoellick

 **Addison-Wesley**

Boston • San Francisco • New York • Toronto • Montreal
London • Munich • Paris • Madrid
Capetown • Sydney • Tokyo • Singapore • Mexico City

The publisher offers discounts on this book when ordered in quantity for special sales. For more information, please contact:

Pearson Education Corporate Sales Division
One Lake Street
Upper Saddle River, NJ 07458
(800) 382-3419
corpsales@pearsontechgroup.com

Visit us on the Web at www.aw.com/cseng/

Library of Congress Cataloging-in-Publication Data

Zoellick, Bill.
    Web engagement : connecting to customers in e-business / Bill Zoellick.
        p. cm. — (Addison Wesley information technology series)
    Includes bibliographical references and index.
    ISBN 0-201-65766-X
    1. Electronic commerce.   2. Internet (Computer network)   3. Business enterprises—Computer networks. I. Title. II. Series.

    HF5548.32.Z64 2000
    658.8'4—dc21   00-028896

ISBN 0-201-65766-X
Text printed on recycled paper
1 2 3 4 5 6 7 8 9 10—MA—0403020100
First printing, May 2000

To Pauline

Contents

Chapter 3 ANSWERING THE BASIC QUESTIONS   31

Chapter 4 GETTING MORE FROM WEBSITE DATA   41

CHAPTER 8 **PERSONALIZATION: USING CUSTOMER DATA 117**

CHAPTER 9 **RESPONDING TO THE CUSTOMER 129**

CHAPTER 10   **CUSTOMERS AS MEMBERS OF GROUPS   149**

CHAPTER 11   **BUILDING PERSONALIZED ENGAGEMENT   175**

Foreword

E-business is different. E-business is so different that, because of it, industries will undergo tectonic shifts that will change the global geology of business—new continents will form with new powers making up the landscape. These shifts in power will be as far-reaching as the recent purchase of Time Warner by AOL. As e-business matures, the companies that understand this new geology—and how to use the natural resources most efficiently and effectively—will emerge as the new leaders. The business models for e-business are such new and unknown territories that no one has a solid grasp of all the possibilities or implications. There is no wide base of experience to go on, and we simply have no way of knowing a priori which models will make the most sense in general or for any particular industry. What works for Amazon may not work for you; in fact it may not work for Amazon next year. In a couple of years all this will become much easier as we learn what works and what doesn't, but businesses that wait are in danger of living off the crumbs of those who understood early and built e-businesses that use the unique characteristics of the web to best advantage.

The *most* unique characteristic of the web is in the way that it changes the relationship between your business and its customers. All business is about customers. It didn't take the web to teach us that. However, the web changes your relationship with customers in two important ways. First, it changes the balance of power between you and the customer, providing the customer with more information and more alternatives. The customer is king as never before. But the changes are not all one-sided. The web gives you new capability as it undermines the old balance of power. Second, the web provides new ways to know and communicate with customers.

These fundamental changes in customer relationship will remain at the core no matter how the geology of e-business develops. They should be considered as first principles of any e-business strategy. The consequences of embracing these changes cut deeper than many businesses realize. A new level of interaction heretofore reserved for the most personal commerce relationships becomes critical to e-commerce success. Customers not only have more power to choose what to buy, but also can choose what information they provide to allow you to market to them. You will not be able to take advantage of the new ways to communicate and know your customers without *engaging* them in a way that encourages them to share information with you.

Many web business strategies begin with a one-sided view of the connection between web data collection and customer relationships, underestimating the power of the customer on the Internet. As a consequence, these companies miscalculate the importance of customer engagement. Mining clickstream and statistical data to push more personalized content at your customers is an important capability. But this one-way push in itself adds little depth to a customer relationship. Any business can collect a certain amount of data without active customer participation, but doing so neither leverages the unique capabilities of the web nor differentiates you from your competition. Your customer's willingness to share additional data about themselves and their needs will determine the value of the relationship you are able to build with them, as well as the value of your business compared to your competition. Engaging your customers requires understanding the new tools and data that are available and applying them in a way that creates and nurtures a new level of trust.

Bill's book is about this kind of web engagement. It is a handbook to help you implement and manage the key changes in the relationship between you and your customer, and is as practical in its delivery as it is important in its message. It builds from a fundamental understanding of the information that can be collected from web customers, to an explanation of what is possible and a clarification of different approaches, and finally to guidance on how to get started. The explication of web data is used as a starting point to elucidate how a web business changes the dynamics of customer relationships. Bill's notion of customer engagement gets at the essence of what makes e-business different.

Frank Gilbane
February 2000

Preface

Success in a web business depends on engaging the customer. This is true to some extent for any business, of course. But it is true for web businesses in new ways, with greater urgency.

The critical importance of connecting to the customer is driven by two facts about the web. The first is that it has shifted the balance of power between buyer and seller in favor of the buyer. This observation has been made so often by so many commentators that it is in danger of no longer being heard. But the sharp edge of this fact is not dulled by its status as an Internet maxim. Build a web business that does not connect with the needs and preferences of customers, that does not delight and serve them, and you will experience new meaning in the phrase "cutting edge."

The second fact that drives web engagement is that the web truly makes possible new levels of attention to customer needs. Unlike print, broadcast, or even direct face-to-face communication with customers, the web is a fully interactive medium that produces its own written record. You can communicate in detail with a customer and retain each of the details. This means that the web enables individual, personalized attention to each customer. Web business customers understand this, and the fact changes their expectations. Engagement is no longer a delightful surprise; it is what it takes to do business.

The Problem

Okay, so customer engagement is a good idea. It is even a necessary part of web business. Seeing this is easy. What is difficult is figuring out how to make it happen.

The difficulty comes from a collision of new technology and new business models. Managing a web business so that it connects with customers requires mastery of both the technology and the business.

If you are running a web business, you need at least a high-level understanding of the nuts and bolts of collecting and using customer data. What is a log file, and what can it tell us about customers? What is a cookie, and why do people worry about cookies? What do they do for my business? What is a collaborative filter? What is involved in implementing personalization on our site? Such general knowledge about tools and options is just as basic as having an understanding of how to interpret inventory information or how to keep track of cost of sales.

At the same time that he or she is learning how to use new tools and interpret new sources of information, a web businessperson has to learn to think about the business in new ways. How can you preserve margins when it is so easy for customers to go to a competitor for a better price? What is the value of the detailed product information that you provide when a customer can easily and anonymously use your information to complete a sale elsewhere? Where does the information that you provide on the web fit into the overall value chain leading to the sale, and how do you ensure that you receive payment for that value?

The Book's Purpose

As of this writing, there is literally no place to go for an understanding of both the technical issues and the business issues underlying customer engagement. This book provides

- A readable, nontechnical introduction to the key tools and issues involved in collecting customer data and making good use of it.
- A discussion of web business strategies and of the ways that they build on customer engagement and are shaped by customer input. The discussion is intended to help you see your business problems in new ways.
- Examples of what other web businesses have tried and learned.
- Concrete suggestions about how to proceed in developing deeper and more informative engagement with your web customers.

Who Should Read This Book

The combination of readable, understandable descriptions of web technologies and consideration of web business strategy makes this book useful for anyone needing a broader view of the options open to a web business. This includes

- Senior managers and strategic planners charged with growing and setting the direction for a web business.
- Corporate executives who need an overview of web business options and a feel for what is possible.
- Information technology managers who need to connect web technology to web business objectives.

Students, entrepreneurs, consultants, and managers who are seeking a way to organize their thinking about customer engagement on the web will find this book both stimulating and, indeed, clarifying. The book brings many different kinds of knowledge and information together into one place. The result is a broad view of a landscape that too often looks like individual rocks and trees.

How the Book Is Organized

Customer engagement moves from the general to the particular. Individual customer engagement works when it builds on the foundation of a sound web business that fits the market it serves. Said another way, before you can engage customers as individual companies or people, you need to engage the market.

Consequently, this book starts by looking at what you can know about your customers as a whole. Chapter 1 begins with a story about the problems encountered by one small business as it moved onto the web. The company's experiences will be familiar to many of you: The initial effect of becoming a web business is a falling-off of revenues. Almost nothing that the management expected to happen does happen. Understanding their web business in the largest sense, as it fits into the market and the aggregate needs of customers, is critical to this company's survival.

Using the problems faced by this small company as a reference point, Chapters 2 through 5 show you how to fill out the "big picture" for your business. These chapters look at the kinds of questions that you can and should be able to answer about your business, and they show you how to use web server log files and other information to get the answers. These chapters also help you see how different web business models need to answer different kinds of questions. The examination of different web business models will help you think more clearly about the primary objectives of your own web business.

Building on the understanding of how to see the big picture of your web business, the book then turns to examination of ways to engage the individual customer. Since engaging individuals works only if you can recognize them, Chapter 6 takes a careful look at the use of "cookies" on websites, which are the most commonly used approach to staying connected to a customer. The discussion of cookies leads naturally to a discussion of privacy and use of customer information. Chapter 7 looks at customer privacy issues in some depth, as there can be no customer engagement without trust.

The focus then shifts to customer engagement in the more particular sense—how to connect with individual companies and people as they do business with you on your site. This exploration begins in Chapter 8 with another story, one that examines what National Semiconductor has done to engage its business customers more closely. Using the National Semiconductor experience as an example of engagement that works, Chapter 9 takes a close look at just how you collect information about individual customers. Then, Chapter 10 shows you how to aggregate these individuals into useful groupings of customers so that you can begin to use the preferences and concerns of the group to drive new kinds of sales.

Finally, Chapter 11 shows you how to tie all the pieces together. Recognizing that the information in the preceding ten chapters is a kind of "kit" of customer engagement tools and practices, this closing chapter outlines a staged development plan for assembling the kit so that the final customer engagement program meets the needs of your company.

B2B and B2C

There is a tendency to think of personalization and customer engagement in terms of businesses that sell directly to end consumers—business-to-consumer (B2C) operations. Although personalization and engagement certainly do matter in B2C businesses, they may be even more important in business-to-business (B2B) operations. The reason is simple: The lifetime value of a B2B customer is typically many times larger than the expected value of a B2C customer. Consequently, it makes good business sense to invest more in strengthening and protecting the engagement.

Throughout this book, I take care to look at tools and practices for both B2B and B2C settings. If there is a bias in my coverage of both of these different kinds of businesses, it is in the direction of showing how to use customer engagement in B2B businesses. The reason for the bias is that so much has been made of personalization and "one-to-one" selling in the consumer realm that I feel a need to work harder to make the case for B2B, as well.

Acknowledgments

The information and advice in this book come from conversations with a great many businesspeople. In some cases, they are people running a very small business, such as an art gallery. In other cases, they are running billion-dollar businesses building huge Internet catalogs. In yet others, they are building an Internet start-up. In all cases, they are concerned about making their web businesses work. The questions and concerns raised by these businesspeople and their desire to know just how to build customer engagement have shaped this book.

A number of consulting engagements have been especially important in providing specific examples for the book. In particular, I would like to thank Phil Gibson of National Semiconductor for the detailed insights into how National Semiconductor has developed personalization for business settings. I also thank Jim Ungerleider, Steve Leavy, and Jim O'Hara of Equilinx for help in understanding their B2B marketplace. Thanks also to Keith Dawson for help in understanding some of the finer points of cookie management.

I would also like to thank the staff at Addison Wesley Longman for their assistance in bringing this book to market. Particular thanks are due to Mary O'Brien, my editor, and to Mariann Kourafas. Thanks are also due to the reviewers who took time from busy schedules to think carefully about what I was trying to do. As they know, they had a substantial impact on the organization and content of this book. I am particularly grateful to Mike McClure, who was busy as VP of Marketing at Marketwave at the time that I came to him, for giving careful consideration, early on, to what was essentially a set of notes. His kind words provided encouragement at a critical point in getting the book going.

I owe thanks to my partners and to the staff at Fastwater LLP for helping keep the business running while I was off working on a book. George Florentine and Lee Fife of Fastwater were particularly helpful in leading me through some of the technical issues discussed in the following pages.

Finally, I am in debt to my family, Pauline, Rachel, and Nicol, for their patience and support. Living with someone who is writing a book means being alone a lot and dealing with a mind that is often elsewhere. Rachel has been through this twice now and, happily, seems to have come through the experience intact both times. Last, I am grateful to my mother for her example of energy, focus, and the will to get things done.

About the Author

Bill Zoellick is a partner at Fastwater LLP, a consulting firm that specializes in helping companies build web businesses. Fastwater's client list includes software companies engaged in e-commerce, financial services companies, application service providers, large business-to-business distributors, and start-up companies wanting to build Internet business marketplaces. Fastwater deals with the technical, business, and marketing issues associated with helping these clients grow and change; Bill's focus is on the business and marketing side of Fastwater's work. The lessons learned from these consulting engagements are reflected in this book.

Bill has also started and managed a variety of businesses and has worked as an industry marketing analyst. Reaching back further in time, Bill used to teach computer science. Bill also coauthored, along with Michael J. Folk and Greg Riccardi, *File Structure in C++, Third Edition,* a widely used textbook on file structures that is also published by Addison-Wesley (1998).

CHAPTER ONE

Becoming a Web Business

Objectives of This Chapter

- Get you thinking about the problems of becoming a web business by taking a close look at the experiences of one particular business.
- Begin to map the route from initial *expectation* to eventual *realization* of the benefits of web business.
- Show the central importance of customer engagement within web businesses.
- Introduce some of the major issues and problems that we will explore over the course of the following chapters.

The web is about promise and possibility. Whether a company is established or is a start-up, putting an offer on the web is filled with the expectation of new customers and new markets. It should be easy, right?

As many companies already know from hard, firsthand experience, there is often a big distance between the expectation and its realization. Helping you cover that distance by engaging the customer is what this book is about. We begin our look at web engagement with the journey of one small company as it started down the road toward becoming a web business.

Build It, They Come, They Leave

The company in this first story is a software company. I began working with the management team to help out with product design issues, but their efforts to move onto the web suddenly got tangled up in their revenue story. Their experiences in dealing with the impacts of the web on revenues and in changing the understanding of their web business provide a good example of the kinds of problems we will be working with throughout the book.

We will call the company "Corporate Publishing Software," or CPS. Over the last decade, CPS has developed a business that consists of selling a mix of software products and professional services. Both the product and the consulting address specialized publishing problems and so sell into a fairly narrow professional market. The service contracts tend to be six- and seven-figure deals that go on for a long time. They are sold by a direct sales force and make up the bulk of the revenue. The software product, despite the fact that it is more tool than application, is one that is easy to use and thus is something that can be sold as a "shrink-wrap" product.

All of this means that CPS is a fairly typical small software company. It has a product but makes most of its money by selling services along with the product. Of course, the margins on product sales are much higher than the margins on services. So, when you look at the numbers, the product sales account for most of the profit. There are literally thousands of small software companies that fit this profile.

Promise: New Growth from the Web

The web appeared to open up a new world of promise for this company. The management at CPS saw three opportunities. First, they could write some web software, and they did, producing a Java-based publishing utility that would be of interest to some of their customers. That wasn't the really exciting thing, however.

The exciting thing was the opportunity to find new customers. One big problem faced by CPS and by most other small software companies is that they do not have ready access to a good software distribution channel. It seemed that the web could change all that. So the second web opportunity that CPS wanted to get hold of was selling its software product directly on the web. Any success there would increase gross margins.

The third benefit that CPS wanted to get from its website was the generation of new sales leads for its services business. Management figured that people coming to the site and downloading or buying product were prospective customers for the full product and services offer.

In sum, CPS wanted to use the web as

- **New product opportunity.** CPS wanted to enter a new market for web publishing.
- **Distribution channel.** CPS would sell product directly on the web.
- **Lead generation.** Website traffic would generate leads that the CPS direct sales force could call on.

CPS set about building the product and the website to reach these objectives. The company retooled its primary product and produced a special web publishing version. Management figured that selling on the web would decrease the cost of sales, which would give them room to adjust price without affecting net margins. They also reasoned that they would sell more product if they reduced the price below $1,000, making more in the long run at the reduced price. So they priced the version of the product that only did web publishing at a couple of hundred dollars and set the price for the full-function, paper, web, and CD-ROM publishing version at just under $1,000.

CPS also wanted leads for its professional services business and correctly recognized that getting name, address, and e-mail address information would be possible only if the company gave the visitor something back in return. So CPS developed a small piece of utility software that it could give away for free. Since the utility program was the sort of thing CPS would be using in its professional services engagements, management figured that people signing up to download the free utility might be good prospects for the broader services offer.

Finally, CPS set about building the website it would need to deliver these products and generate these leads. It hired a large PR agency with a website division, paying them tens of thousands of dollars to design a visually attractive website. The site consisted of a home page that served as a jumping-off point to information about the company, information about products, news about CPS, job information, and so on. The usual stuff. The home page itself consisted of a visually attractive, but not meaningful, image and some general information about the company and about the changes taking place in publishing.

So, after spending some serious money, measured in CPS's terms, and retooling its offer, CPS was in the web business. The site was up. CPS waited for things to start happening.

Perplexity: Running a Web Business

After a month, it was clear that the site was not working as expected. Product revenues were the one thing that the company was tracking, and there wasn't much product being sold on the web. That, combined with the drop in the price of the product, resulted in an actual decline in product revenues. CPS acquired some inexpensive traffic analysis software and found that the site was drawing only tens of visitors per day rather than the hundreds that CPS had expected.

CPS went back to the PR firm and asked for help in increasing traffic. It spent another few tens of thousands of dollars and came away with a site that was filled with words and metadata (terms describing the page that are not visible to the reader but that search engines see) that it hoped would bring in visitors from search engines. The company also managed to get mentions and links in a number of technology publications on the web and from a couple of larger corporate sites.

These changes brought results. Traffic increased into the range of hundreds of visitors a day. Product sales also increased, but not in proportion to the traffic. At least, however, product revenues were now back to what they were before the web initiative. CPS was also getting a lot of activity in the free-download area and was collecting the names, company affiliations, and e-mail addresses of everyone who downloaded the free product.

At this point, CPS moved from panic to puzzlement. The site no longer felt like a mistake, but it also was not meeting the objectives that CPS had identified at the outset. The company was not selling much of the new web software—in fact, most sales were still of the older publishing product. It had not succeeded in turning the web into a new, much more effective channel. It was acquiring a good number of names but was finding out that not all of these names were actually good sales leads. It seemed as though the quality of the leads might even be below that of names from business cards dropped in a bowl at the CPS booth at trade shows—which is to say that the quality was quite low.

Surprise: Seeing the Web Business as Others See You

It is valuable to step back from the details of the CPS story for a moment and look at the pattern of the company's response. It is a pattern that most companies go through; perhaps even your own company has tried it. The management at CPS started out with a set of expectations about what participation in web business would do for them. They were, of course, positive expectations. When, as is often the case, the expectations did not materialize, the company tinkered with the website. The tinkering was not informed by any careful analysis and was really just a second shot at the target.

Like CPS, most companies find that the second shot falls short. Maybe it is a bit closer, maybe nothing changes, but the clear fact is that something is wrong, and management does not know how to fix it. It is usually at this point that a company decides to take a more analytical approach to the problem, looking carefully at what is actually happening on the website. This is precisely what CPS did.

The first question that management asked was, Who is visiting our site? This is certainly an important step beyond simply asking, How many visitors? It gets at the idea of "quality" and at the problem of identifying the "right kind" of visitors—the ones that could turn into leads. CPS was gathering good identifying information about the people who were downloading the free software. There are always at least a few people who provide false identifying information, but it appeared that most of the names and company affiliations were genuine. Since CPS was trying to understand the overall operation of the site, however, it really wanted to know more about the general visitor profile, including the people who were not downloading a free development tool.

Like most companies, CPS found to its frustration that the answer to the *who* question was more elusive than the answer to the *how many* question. The company was able to get only the most general, and not very useful, profiles of visitors from the data collected in its log files. For example, the data showed that most of the visitors were from the United States and that there were visitors from some big companies. But details about the visitors were hard to come by. Contrary to the popular impression that the Internet is a way to learn all kinds of things about the buying habits of customers, the CPS website data were frustratingly unrevealing.

Having found that the *who* question was not answerable in a way that helped them understand why their web business was not working as they wanted it to, management next turned to asking, What are visitors actually doing when they come to our site? This turned out to be a much more productive question because it was one on which the CPS website data could shed some light.

The data contained a number of important facts about visitor behavior:

- Most of the traffic coming to the site was not from other sites or the result of searches but consisted of people directly keying in the URL for the CPS home page.

- Most visitors who did come from other sites were following links to the free software download, posted on sites that were directories of free publishing utilities.
- Very few visitors came as a result of search queries using the terms that CPS had, at considerable expense, worked into its site.
- A very large proportion of the visitors never moved beyond the home page.
- Those who did go beyond the home page typically went straight to the free download.
- Customers who did buy the actual product went directly to the page where they placed an order. In general, these customers preferred to have the product sent to them rather than downloading it.
- Virtually no visitors were looking at CPS corporate information, product descriptions, news, or other information on the site.

These facts about CPS's visitors were both surprising and troubling. One of the most fundamental assumptions underlying CPS's model for its new web business was that it would be able to effect a kind of "cross-selling." Simply stated, the assumption had been that people drawn to the site by the free offer would find other things of interest on the site, would perhaps buy the revenue-producing product, and would maybe be decent leads for the services business. The fact that the people coming for the free download went straight to their goal, without looking at anything else on the site, raised doubts about the validity of that assumption in the minds of even the most optimistic managers at CPS.

The website log file data contained other less direct implications that were, if anything, even more troubling. CPS, like any other business, feels that what it is doing is important, valuable, and interesting. Experience over years of face-to-face selling had shown CPS that customers and prospects understood the value that CPS offered and reflected CPS's own sense of value in the market. CPS customers liked CPS and generally regarded it as an interesting, innovative little company. The more that management looked at the log file analysis, however, the more it seemed that the typical CPS website visitor had no inkling of this value and perhaps couldn't care less. They were coming only for the free stuff.

There is a lot of free stuff on the web. Some of it is good; some is not. Since the CPS stuff was good, word was apparently getting around: "These folks have a good free utility. Get it." For most visitors, CPS was a place to get something for free, and nothing more. It was as if the web visitors just didn't understand.

A Continuing Story

The CPS story does not come to any nice, tidy conclusion because the company is still working on figuring out its web business. The good news is that it has been acquired by a larger software company under terms that pleased the stockholders. But the acquisition has kept CPS's product lines intact, and the company still engaged in learning how to use the web effectively.

Using the information that emerged from the analysis of its website data, CPS is now making the path to the free software less direct. The goal is to make sure that anyone downloading the utilities has at least been exposed to a short description of what CPS is all about and what else it offers.

CPS is also at work on some technical papers that should be of interest to the visitors coming for the free software and that will be available with the free utility and perhaps even tied to it. The technical papers should allow CPS to do a better job of expressing the value that it offers, beyond free software. CPS is also reworking the home page, finding a way to make it less of a dead end for people typing in the CPS URL.

Just as important as the changes to the site are the changes in the web business model. CPS has a clearer notion that people providing names and e-mail addresses are a long way from being leads. CPS is now tying the website registration data into its sales force automation system so that it can do a better job of identifying visitors who are more likely to be good prospects for a full offer.

Lessons from CPS

The CPS story illustrates many of the important problems that companies encounter on the web. First, and perhaps most important, CPS's experience underscores the fact that your company's identity on the web may be very different from the identity that you project in other settings. This is, in a way, a kind of reversal of the Peter Steiner cartoon about how "On the Internet, nobody knows you're a dog." It turns out that the separation of your Internet identity from your nonwired identity cuts both ways. Particularly if you are a smaller company or a new company, all that your website visitors know about you is what they find on your site. In CPS's case, the Internet decided that CPS was a place that provides free software. It is usually hard to accept the web's judgment about your identity—most companies would like it to be otherwise—but the sooner you figure out who you are on the Internet, the sooner you can go about either taking advantage of that identity or changing it.

"On the Internet, nobody knows you're a dog."

The second lesson from the CPS story is the importance of simple website log file analysis for unwinding this matter of your web business identity. In almost all companies, it takes a while for management to move beyond using log files simply as a way of keeping score: "Do we have more visitors this month than last month?" As CPS found, it is much more important to know how customers are actually using your site rather than simply keeping track of how many of them there are. As we will see in more detail in Chapter 2, log files do a good job of holding up a mirror to your site so that you can see your business as visitors see it.

Along with the good things that log files can do, the CPS story illustrates some of their limitations. In particular, they are not much help in identifying or profiling customers. In Chapter 2 we will find out why, and in subsequent chapters we will look at ways to do a much better job of collecting such information. We will also look at how you can get to know your customers as individuals and develop truly personalized engagement with them.

Another important lesson from the CPS story is that it can be very difficult to transfer a visitor's attention from the things that brought that visitor to your site to content and activities that are more central to your business. This is what we called CPS's "cross-sell" problem: Having "sold" the visitor on the free software, CPS wanted to also get the visitor's attention for revenue-producing product and services. In CPS's case, there were probably several reasons why the cross-sell was not working. The most obvious reason, as the log file analysis showed, was that the site was initially constructed so that the cross-sell message was never presented to the visitor as he or she made a beeline for the free utility.

There are often even deeper problems in making a cross-sell work. A cross-sell depends on connecting the thing that a customer is buying with something else that the buyer wants. Pulling this off requires understanding the behaviors of buyers as members of groups. It is by looking at what the group is doing that you can begin to make projections about the preferences of individual buyers. One of the classic examples of this is the discovery by convenience stores that they could sell more beer if they put it near the disposable diapers. Fathers coming in for diapers would see the beer and would often suddenly decide to pick up a six-pack. The behavior of the group became a good predictor for individual behavior. In the latter chapters of this book, we will show you how to use data collected from your customers to form such groups and to automate cross-selling. (Note, by the way, that as you translate the diapers-and-beer story into web business, it is probably just as important *not* to associate diapers and beer when the customer is female. The website needs to respond to the actual interests of the individual visitor rather than to some general notion of what might work.)

Web Engagement

Understanding how customers see you, knowing what they are doing on your site, understanding their individual needs, and supporting cross-selling by grouping customers together are all dimensions of customer engagement on the web. CPS managed to move only a short way down the road to customer engagement in the part of its story recounted in this first chapter. The company came to understand something about how its web customers perceived and used its business and is just beginning to learn more about its customers as individual buyers. The next steps, still in the future for CPS, will provide the company with opportunities to begin providing personalized service to customers, collecting information about individual customer needs, and learning to respond to those needs through its web business.

Engaging the customer in this way, using the Internet to create a more closely coupled relationship, is not just a good idea. Over the next few years, it will become an indispensable part of CPS's ability to sell its products, provide services, and grow its business. Perhaps the most powerful fact about the Internet is that it has changed the relationship between buyers and sellers, giving the buyer more choice, more information, and more control than ever before. CPS, like other businesses, will need to continue to learn to use the web as a way to engage these newly empowered customers. Done right, the opportunity for engagement can rearrange the market and open new opportunities for CPS and its new parent company.

The journey from the initial high expectations in a web business ("This will be easy. It is like printing money. Just think of all the potential customers!") to the reality of making the business work is usually a long one. Engaging customers—getting them to come to your web business and then binding them to you—is an important part of completing this journey. The following chapters will show you how to learn about your customers and how to connect to their needs as companies and as individual buyers.

Key Ideas

- Most web businesses are not yet quite sure of their destination and are flying blind as they head there, gathering and using only the most basic information about what visitors are doing on their sites.
- Web visitors, not you, decide what good your web business is to them.
- Basic site statistics are essential—there is no other way to understand how your business is being regarded and used.
- Key questions are *what* visitors are doing and *who* they are. The *who* question is harder to answer than the *what* question.
- Understanding what works and what doesn't is a stepwise process.
- Creating an effective crossover between free offers on your site and your revenue-producing business can be very difficult and depends on making sure the prospects for the free offer are members of the same group that would be interested in the product you have for sale.
- Customer engagement—understanding the needs of different groups of customers and meeting those needs—is essential to success on the web.

CHAPTER TWO

Getting the Big Picture

Objectives of This Chapter

- List a few of the key questions that any web business should be able to answer about itself and about its relationship to customers.
- Show how log file analysis and other, similar approaches can help answer these questions.
- Provide a simple explanation of what is in a log file and about how the information can be used.

A Few Basic Questions

CPS's experiences as it began the journey toward becoming a web business are not at all unusual. Like many companies starting a web business, CPS did not bother to design a plan for collecting and analyzing website data as it built the site. The company was so sure of its success on the web that it even dropped the price on products, confident that the decreased revenues on each sale would be made up by increased sales volume.

Because CPS had not built monitoring capability into its site at the outset, the first strong signal that things were not working out as planned was pretty painful: Revenues were down. It was only then that CPS began looking at traffic and discovered that there was not enough of it. The site redesign followed, and traffic picked up. However, even with increased traffic, the business was not performing as expected. It was only then that CPS began log file analysis in earnest, trying to understand what was going on.

In short, like many companies, CPS "backed into" log file analysis, discovering what the data collected on its website could reveal only after the company had a real problem. Not surprisingly, it is much better to plan on doing the analysis at the outset. Here is a list of four simple but very important questions that anyone running a web business should be able to answer:

1. How much use is the website getting?
2. What parts of the site get the most use? What is it that visitors are interested in?
3. How do people find out about the site? Where are they coming from?
4. Is the site functional in terms of the intended purpose? Are people using it as we would expect them to?

These are very fundamental questions. Yet it is surprising that many web businesses have difficulty answering them in a convincing way. When I meet with managers to talk about their web businesses, I find that as soon as I press on these questions, asking specifics, there is usually little there that the company can count on.

Happily, it is possible to get answers, with supporting information, for each of these questions through basic log file analysis. In this chapter, we look at what is inside a log file that you can use to answer these questions. You need to know what log files contain in order to know what you do with them; the next dozen or so pages tell you that. Then, in Chapter 3, we will return to our four basic questions and will show you how to develop answers and tie them into your business.

Where Do Log Files Come From?

When visitors come to your website, they interact with software known as a *web server*. The web server software is usually running on a piece of hardware that is also called a *server*. We are interested in the software server, not the hardware server.

The browser running on the visitor's computer delivers requests to your web server. If the request is a legal one that can be fulfilled, the server finds the page, image, or other file that was requested and sends it back to the browser. If you have a busy site that is handling a lot of requests, you probably have a number of web servers that are running at the same time, sharing the work of handling the requests.

As each of the servers goes about its job of responding to requests, it writes out a log that contains a record of every request that it receives, along with information about how it handles the request. It records things such as whether it

---

Technical Note: Log Files, Network Sniffers, and Plug-ins

Before we dive into the details of what is inside a log file, we should prepare you for the fact that some website analysis tools emphasize the use of network sniffers rather than just focusing on analysis of log files. The difference, in plain English, is that whereas the *log file* is written out by the web server as it goes about its job of sending files back to visitors, a *network sniffer* is actually a separate piece of hardware that is sitting on the network, between the web servers and the visitors, looking at each packet that is sent back and forth.

As you look at web analysis products, it is certain that you will eventually talk to a salesperson who tells you that it is silly to use log files and that what you really need is a network sniffer. You will encounter others who tell you that sniffers are bad and that you should use log files. Yet others will talk about a third approach based on *plug-ins* to the web server, whereby a separate program works in conjunction with your web server to provide monitoring capability. Our goal here is to ensure that such assertions don't confuse you.

The most crucial thing for you to remember is that most of the important capabilities (and most of the important limitations) that we describe for log files also apply to the data from network sniffers or plug-ins. Yes, there are differences among the approaches. For instance, using a sniffer might be attractive if you have many web servers because it might be able to collect information for all the servers at once. Choosing the right approach can, in fact, be important. Your technical team can help make such a choice. The important issue, however, from a business management perspective, is what these devices and tools can tell you, not how they work. Each approach is capable of answering the kinds of general questions posed at the start of this chapter, and each suffers from some of the same limitations, which we are about to discuss, in knowing very much about actual individual visitors.

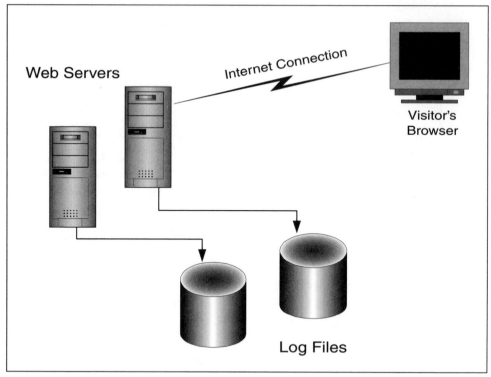

Figure 2–1 Web servers producing separate log files

sends the file back successfully, cannot find the file, declines access to the file because the requestor does not have permission to see it, and so on. This request-by-request record of activity is the "log file" that we use for analyzing site activities. Unless some administrator in your organization has taken the unusual step of explicitly telling the web server to *not* record all of its activities, log files recording your website activity are stored away someplace on your system, one for each server that is supporting your website, as shown in Figure 2–1.

What Is in a Log File?

A log file is made up of line after line of text—text that is directly readable by humans. Because we can read log file records, understanding the structure of log files is much more straightforward than, say, understanding the structure of a relational database. We can simply scan through the file and look at a few records.

The Content of a Log File Record

Most web servers can write records in a format known as the *Common Log File* (CLF) format. Different servers may extend this format in different ways, but looking at the CLF is a good place to start in answering the question of what is in a log file. Here is a CLF entry that records a single event on a website at a company that publishes market research information for a set of subscribers. It is actually a single line in the log file; we break it up here for readability:

```
207.94.105.77 - - [27/Jun/1999:12:09:53 -0700]
   "GET /members/NEPs/ HTTP/1.1" 200 3528
```

Let's take a close look at this record, field by field, to see what it contains. (We are not trying to turn you into a technology wizard. But, unless you know what kinds of things are collected in a log file, it is very difficult to make intelligent judgments about what you can and cannot do with the data that you have been collecting.) Table 2–1 contains a description of each of the fields in this record.

If you think about these fields critically, in terms of our goal of obtaining some understanding of what is happening on a website, it appears that there are only three useful pieces of information in a log file record. The first is the IP address of the machine that is being used by the person making the request. It is useful because it might be able to tell us something about who is visiting the site. The second is the identity of the requested page, which tells us what the visitor is coming to see. The third is the timing of the request, which can help us relate this request to others, perhaps enabling us to observe the progress of a visit.

This is not to say that the other fields are of no use at all. Some of the fields are very useful in monitoring operational aspects of a site. For instance, if a lot of people are requesting a page that doesn't exist on the site, this problem shows up as a record with a return status of 404, indicating that the requested page was not found. If a log file contains return status codes of 404, it is usually because links are broken, pointing to pages that have moved or that have been taken from the site. The log file helps in detecting and fixing such problems. This is an important function, but it is not the kind of thing that sheds much light on the larger questions of how the site is working in the context of your business.

Records Associated with the Initial Request

The NEPs directory, referenced in the log file record that we have just examined, is a location on this company's site where it publishes case studies of web

Table 2–1 Contents of a Basic Log File Record

Contents	Field Name	Description
207.94.105.77	remotehost	IP address of the host computer used to send the request.
- (first hyphen)	rfc931	Remote login name of the user. This is typically not available, which is what the hyphen tells us in this case.
- (second hyphen)	authuser	Username of an authenticated user. This is not generally useful because most sites use more sophisticated login methods.
[27/Jun/1999:12:09:53-0700]	date	Date and time of the request, measured to seconds.
"GET /members/NEPs/ HTTP/1.1"	request	HTTP request, as it came from the client. In this case, we can see that the main index page within the NEPs directory ("/members/NEPs/") was requested. By convention, if a request is for a directory rather than for a specific file, the server returns the "index.html" file in the directory if such a file exists.
200	status	HTTP status returned to the client. "200" means the request was filled successfully.
3528	Bytes	Number of bytes returned.

businesses. The record tells us that somebody associated with the IP address 207.94.105.77 requested the index page to this directory a little after noon on June 27, 1999.

What do we make of that? Not much, as you might have guessed. A single log file record is just not very interesting. It takes an aggregation of these records, over time, to show us anything useful. So let's look at some more records in this log file.

It turns out that the next three entries in the log file are from someone with the same IP address and so are probably tied to the record we have just examined. They look like this:

```
207.94.105.77 - - [27/Jun/1999:12:09:54 -0700]
    "GET /style/display.css HTTP/1.1" 200 2803
207.94.105.77 - - [27/Jun/1999:12:09:55 -0700]
    "GET /images/logo_small.gif HTTP/1.1" 200 1488
207.94.105.77 - - [27/Jun/1999:12:09:55 -0700]
    "GET /images/bullet7.gif HTTP/1.1" 200 140
```

These three records tell us that, immediately after the request for the index page from the NEPs subdirectory, the visitor's web browser made requests for the related style sheet, for the GIF (graphics interface format) file containing the company logo, and for another GIF file containing an image of a bullet. From the descriptions of these files, it is probably already clear that these were not things that the visitor explicitly requested. Instead, the visitor's browser requested these pages because the first page—the one that the visitor actually asked for—makes use of these other files to create the final presentation.

For our purposes, these additional records do not provide any useful information: We already know that the pages use style sheets and bullets. However, the log file methodically records every request received by the web server, and those requests include not only the actual primary web pages on a site but also all the other files used to construct those pages. For sites that use many images and complex page construction, the ratio of requests for such supporting files to actual pages seen by the visitor is often 10 to 1, or greater.

Some Implications

We have just started our look at the contents of log files but have already uncovered a number of facts about them that are of interest to managers and staff who are using log files to learn more about their web businesses:

- **Log files are low-level records.** They capture activity at a very detailed level. This can be useful. For example, if we have a GIF image associated with an advertisement, the log file can tell us how many times that particular image has been delivered. But it also means that much of the information in a log file is not very useful for understanding what visitors are actually doing on the website.

- **Log files are big.** Rather than being tightly compressed records designed solely for machine storage and retrieval, they are made up of verbose, human-readable records that use a relatively large amount of space to give us a few pieces of basic information. The enormous size of the log files—often ranging into *gigabytes* per day on a busy site—can make them very difficult to use. Certainly, if you have a number of geographically dispersed web servers, sending the log files around can take a lot of time. One financial services company with servers in the United States and in Europe literally spends over an hour each night just transporting the files to a central location for processing.

- **There are different ways to count.** We can look at "hits" (requests) and count every record in a log file, or we can simply count "page views." The sample records we examined earlier make up four requests for files but only a single page view. To understand data about a site's activity, you must know how the counting is done.

Perhaps the most important implication of these observations is that we will need to look at entire sequences of log file records to get a useful, interesting picture of what is happening. A single record or a small collection of records doesn't tell us much.

Following the Actions of a Single Visitor

Picking through all the graphics, style sheet references, and other calls to the web server to reconstruct a visitor's activity can be an arduous task. On an active site, where many requests from different users are coming in all the time, often during the same second, there can be thousands of records separating the trail of different page views associated with a single user. This is what log file analysis programs do, and it is a much better job for software than for human readers. But in order to get a better understanding of just how the records of a log file come together to provide a bigger picture of what is going on, let's follow the progress of our visitor from IP address 207.94.105.77 on June 27, 1999.

Here is the sequence of requests that followed the visitor's initial entry onto the site. These records were extracted from the list of hundreds of other records that document the activity on this company's site for this period of about four minutes of elapsed time. We have removed all the extraneous calls for images and other related files (these records show the pages actually requested by the visitor), and we have trimmed off the tail of the records to make them easier to read:

```
207.94.105.77 - - [27/Jun/1999:12:10:16 -0700]
   "GET / . . .
207.94.105.77 - - [27/Jun/1999:12:10:45 -0700]
   "GET /membership.html . . .
207.94.105.77 - - [27/Jun/1999:12:11:21 -0700]
   "GET /members/NEPs/index.html . . .
207.94.105.77 - - [27/Jun/1999:12:12:04 -0700]
   "GET /members/rapids/index.html . . .
207.94.105.77 - - [27/Jun/1999:12:13:43 -0700]
   "GET /members/rapids/v1-6_dist-channel.html . . .
```

Following the visitor's movement around the site is easier if you know something about the purpose and structure of this company's website. A primary function of the site is to deliver research and analysis to the company's subscribers. A second, equally important goal is to attract new subscribers. Hence the site is a mix of content that is reserved for subscribers only and of free-sample content that is available to anybody. Like most websites, this one is organized into a set of directories and files, as shown in Figure 2–2.

Using this diagram of the site's structure, let's follow this visitor's progress around the site, as recorded in the log file. We know from our earlier discussion that he or she entered the site by first requesting the index page in the "/members/NEPs" subdirectory. (This fact is interesting in itself. How did the visitor jump onto the site at this point? Later we will find out how the log file can help us answer this question, too.) This index page contains a list of the case studies offered by the company.

The next significant log file entry related to this visitor, ignoring all the requests for images, style sheets, and so on, is the "GET /" request. Remember that if there is a file named "index.html" in a directory, a request for the directory itself, by convention, retrieves the index.html file. The index.html file that is in the root (home) directory of a site is typically the "home page" for the site. So our visitor has followed a link on the NEPs index page to go back and have a look at the company's home page.

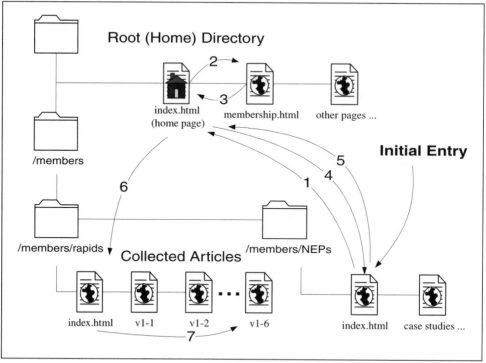

Figure 2–2 Structure of website visited by 207.94.105.77

The next page request in the log file from this visitor is this one:

```
207.94.105.77 - - [27/Jun/1999:12:10:45 -0700]
    "GET /membership.html . . .
```

This request comes after the visitor has spent just under 30 seconds looking over the home page. In this case, the visitor is following a link from the home page to a description of the benefits of becoming a subscriber to the company's publications. A good sign. Maybe the company has a potential new subscriber in the wings.

The next log file entry for this visitor occurs 36 seconds later and looks like this:

```
207.94.105.77 - - [27/Jun/1999:12:11:21 -0700]
    "GET /members/NEPs/index.html . . .
```

This is a request, once again, for the index page for the case study information—the page that the visitor first looked at when coming to the site.

This particular request illustrates an interesting fact about log files because it just so happens that, on this site, there is no direct link from the membership page ("membership.html") that connects to the NEPs index page. As indicated by arrow 3 in Figure 2–2, the visitor has to return to the home page before following a link (arrow 4) down to the NEPs index. So why isn't there a log file entry that tells us that the visitor went back to the home page?

The answer is that most web browsers are set up to *cache* pages. When you use the "Back" command on your browser, it typically does not go out to the website to request the page you want to return to; instead, it just displays the page from the local cache. The important lesson here, for our purposes, is that the log file does not necessarily show us everything that the visitor did or experienced. It only records requests that reach the site's web server. This can become a real issue when there is a *proxy server* managed by a big service provider such as AOL that sits between your site and a visitor. The server is helping out by caching many pages in order to speed up performance and cut down on traffic across the Internet. On busy sites, where many visitors might request the same page over a short period of time, it could turn out that many of the requests are taken care of by the proxy server without ever reaching your site. The result is that there would be many page requests that never show up in your log file.

The next entry in the log file associated with our visitor is as follows:

```
207.94.105.77 - - [27/Jun/1999:12:12:04 -0700]
    "GET /members/rapids/index.html . . .
```

Once again, there is no direct path from the "/members/NEPs/index.html" page to the "/members/rapids/index.html" page, so we can surmise that the user again hit the "Back" button to return to the home page before heading down to the page in the "rapids" directory that contains a list of all the newsletters that are on the site. As on the index of the case studies, some of the newsletters are available as samples to any visitor, and others are reserved only for subscribers.

This visitor is certainly spending a fair amount of time wandering around on the site and looking at the publications that the company offers. Perhaps we do have a potential subscriber here. The next request from this visitor, which comes after about 40 seconds of reading the summaries of the different newsletters, is for one specific issue of the newsletter that is available for free:

```
207.94.105.77 - - [27/Jun/1999:12:13:43 -0700]
    "GET /members/rapids/v1-6_dist-channel.html . . .
```

Sadly, from the standpoint of the company's wanting to sign up more subscribers, this is the last record in the log file from the visitor with IP address 207.94.105.77. It is a little like following a set of footsteps in the snow and then having them end, as if the person suddenly flew away. Perhaps the visitor read the article on distribution channels in volume 1, issue 6, of the newsletter and found the information that he or she wanted. Perhaps the visitor printed out the information. Maybe he or she disliked the site and left in frustration. The log file doesn't say.

Questions about Visitors

Despite the unanswered questions, there is something akin to intimacy about being able to reconstruct one individual's actions in the way that we just have. The log file tells us that someone came to this company's site just after noon on June 27, 1999, and allows us to reconstruct this person's visit, seeing just what he or she was looking at and making some pretty good guesses about how long the person spent reviewing each page.

This is potentially useful information, just taken as it is. Aggregated over many visitors, it would allow us to answer questions such as these:

- Which pages are people visiting the most?
- Which pages do people spend the most time on?
- Which pages never get visited? (This raises the question, Why not? Too hard to find?)
- Which pages get visited for only a brief moment? (This suggests a need for redesign.)
- Do certain pages tend to be the last pages during a visit? (Again, why? They answer everybody's questions? Make people want to go away?)

These are the "easy" questions, in the sense that they are simple to answer just by tabulating some frequency counts from the log file. There are also some hard questions. Unfortunately, it is the hard questions that are often very interesting:

- How do visitors find our site? Where did they go next?
- Who is this person with the IP address of 207.94.105.77? Where does he or she work? Is this a potential customer? A competitor?
- Does this visitor ever return? (Maybe when the visitor does return, he or she does, in fact, subscribe. Maybe we would find that the pattern is that people visit a few times before getting the authorization to spend the money for a subscription.)

These questions are doubly interesting because looking at the answers opens up a number of new insights into the capabilities and limitations of log files.

Where Do They Come From?

One of the intriguing things about the visit that we just reconstructed was that it did not start at the home page. This is interesting because it suggests that this visitor probably did not reach the site just by typing in a URL such as "www.companyname.com." Doing that just takes people to the home page. This visitor entered at a location buried within the site: "www.companyname.com/ members/NEPs." This suggests that he or she probably came into the site by following a link from someplace else.

Fortunately, this is not just something about which we have to make suppositions. In addition to the basic, core log file information that we looked at in Table 2–1, there are log file *extensions* that can collect additional information of interest. Most web servers are already set up to support a small, generally accepted set of these extensions. In other words, the extended data-collection capabilities are already "in the box." You simply need to ask your system administrator to switch on these extended capabilities.

Referrer Information in Log Files

One of the most useful extensions to the standard fields in a log file record is the ability to capture the URL that was being visited before the jump to the current page. Put another way, if a visitor came to a page on your site by following a link, it is possible to identify the origination point of that link. This field is called the *referrer* information since it identifies where the reference to the current page came from. (People don't always follow links to move around on the web. Often they type in a URL directly or use a URL stored in a bookmark. When they do this, there is no referrer, and so the referrer field is empty. Referrer information is available only when someone clicks on a link to move from one page to another.)

It is easy to see how this information is useful. We noticed earlier that the visitor from IP address 207.94.105.77 came into the site without first visiting the home page, suggesting that he or she came in using a link from another site. Here is the referrer entry that tells us just where this visitor came from:

```
http://www.kmworld.com/newestlibrary/1998/november98/
    theknowlmktplc.cfm -> /members/NEPs/index.html
```

Technical Note: Referrer Information

Different web servers use different methods for recording referrer information, sometimes even keeping it in a separate file. So the actual textual information in your log file might not look quite the same as what we are showing you here.

The good news is that commercial log file analysis programs already know about these different formats and are set up to handle them. All you need to know is what referrer information is and how you can use it. Leave the details to your software package.

This referrer information tells us that the visitor jumped to the NEPs index page by following a link found on a page on the *KM World* site. When we go to that address, we do, in fact, find an article that references a case study found on the NEPs index page. Clearly, this is important information. We can find out which other sites are bringing us traffic.

Search Terms Used to Reach Your Site

The referrer information can go beyond telling you about static links to your site, like the one we just examined. It can also help you find out when people are coming to your site through the use of a search engine and can even tell you which search terms they used. Here is a link to the company's site coming from AltaVista:

```
http://www.altavista.com/cgi-bin/query?pg=q&kl=
    XX&q=%22personalization+and+customization%22 -›/
    members/NEPs/BayNetworks.htm
```

This referrer entry tells us that this visitor (a different one) came to the site to look at a case study contained in the file "BayNetworks.htm." This person found the case study by doing a search on AltaVista, using the phrase "personalization and customization." The reason that log files can capture this kind of information is that search engines encode a visitor's query as parameters at the end of a URL. Different search engines use the parameters in different ways, but since there are only a relatively small number of widely used search engines, commercial log file analysis tools are already set up to handle the query decoding for each of the popular search services.

Knowing which search terms people are using to reach your site can tell you a great deal about how visitors "see" your site. This is directly connected to the question of your company's "identity" on the Internet. Like CPS back in Chapter 1, you may find that visitors are coming to your site for reasons that are quite different from the ones you had in mind when you built the site. Using log files to collect information about which terms are used most frequently in reaching your site can help you understand your Internet identity, as seen by your visitors.

Other Log File Extensions

Referrer entries are only one of a number of extensions to the basic information that is generally available in the Common Log File (CLF) format that is supported by all web servers. A number of other extensions are widely supported both by web servers and by the log file analysis tools that you use to digest and interpret the log file information. These extensions include

- **Information about the visitor's browser.** It is sometimes useful to know which browsers, in which versions, are used most often in visiting your site. The log file can collect such information.
- **The operating system used by visitors.** Most web servers and analysis packages make it easy to collect information about how many of your visitors are using Windows 95, Windows 98, Linux, UNIX, and so on.
- **The amount of time required to respond to a request.** This information is useful if you are concerned about performance issues.
- **Information about cookies.** Cookies can be a valuable tool for keeping track of visitor information. We will look at them in detail later. Your log file and your analysis tools can be set up to keep track of cookie information in the log file records.

Although the details about these extensions can be left to the technical people in your organization, it is important for anyone running a web business to have an idea of what is readily available. In our work teaching about how companies can use website data, we have encountered managers who have been told by their IT staff, for example, that it is simply not possible to collect information about which web browsers are used in visiting a site. It is important for managers to have a good feel for what is easy and what is hard. Collecting the kinds of information just listed is easy.

Technical Note: Custom Extensions

Strictly speaking, it is possible for a programmer to add extensions to log files at will, so long as there is some way to capture the data that is to be placed in the extended record. One example of such a custom extension might be an added field to hold information about a visitor that is retrieved from a database, assuming use of a login procedure in which the visitor identifies himself or herself.

However, since most businesses use a commercial log file analysis package to summarize and analyze the contents of a log file, owner-built custom extensions also require modifications in the use of the analysis program. Most high-quality analysis tools do provide ways to make such modifications, enabling use of custom extensions.

In practice, though, most companies do not use custom, one-off extensions. The reason is that there are usually more efficient ways to manage and store such information other than sticking it in the ASCII log file, where the problem is already that the log file is too big. Such problems are more often addressed through the use of a user ID, usually collected through the use of cookies, that is placed in the log file record. This ID is then used as an index into a database where other information is stored. We will discuss such methods in more detail in Chapter 6 on cookies.

Summary

We have covered a lot of ground in this chapter, putting in place the foundation for succeeding chapters that look at how we use the information collected in log files. A quick summary is in order here, however, that pulls together all of this information before we move on.

Log files are written by web servers, recording each request received by the web server. If you have multiple web servers, you have multiple log files. The information recorded in the log file includes the time that the request was received, the IP address of the browser sending the request, the file that was requested, and the web server's response to the request. In addition, log files can tell you things such as which page a visitor was looking at before linking to a new page, what search terms were used in a query leading to a page on your site, and which browser a visitor is using.

Because it can take many requests to get all the files needed to assemble a single web page, the information in the log files is at a finer level of detail than is typically useful for analyzing website performance from a business perspective. One consequence of this is that the log files require extensive processing in order to create the kind of higher-level picture of activity that is actually useful for answering business questions. Another consequence is that log files can be quite large, even if they are holding only a day or so of information, a situation that is compounded by the fact that log files are wordy in order to be human-readable.

Because they capture information about which pages are being viewed on your site, when you aggregate the results over many visitors, log files do a very good job of providing a useful picture of activity on your site. Questions that are easy to answer from log file information include

- Approximately how many visits does your site receive per day or week?
- Is the number of visits increasing? Does it increase or decrease in response to other activities, such as e-mail solicitations, advertisements, publication announcements, and other promotions?
- Are there time-of-day, day-of-week, or day-of-month patterns to traffic on your site?
- What other sites contain links that bring people to your site?
- What search terms most often bring people to your site?
- Which pages do people look at the most?
- Which pages are viewed least often?
- Are there broken links on your site where visitors follow links into missing pages?
- How often are particular ads or other images delivered by your server?
- What browsers are most often used in viewing your site?
- Which companies visit your site most often?
- Approximately how many users come from North America? From Europe? From elsewhere?

With the addition of cookies and connections to registration information, which we will explore in subsequent chapters, log files can become the basis for answering even more interesting questions, such as whether the behavior of returning visitors differs from that of new visitors.

Key Ideas

- Log files are a key part of your web business analysis landscape. Getting a good understanding of what they contain and what they can and cannot be used to do is critical to your having realistic expectations about what is hard and what is easy when it comes to web business analysis.
- Log files are detailed. Getting information out of the detail requires processing and analysis using some kind of analysis tool.
- Log files are good for presenting general frequency counts about activity on the site, such as counts of which pages are visited most, which other sites most often bring visitors to your site, and so on.
- Because log files are so big and so detailed, the processing costs associated with turning log files into something more useful can be substantial. If your site is a busy one, ad hoc analysis is usually out of the question. You should approach log file analysis with a clear idea of what questions you need to answer.

Further Reading

One reason that we have taken the time to treat log file records in such careful detail is that, in my company's consulting work, we found that there are essentially no good discussions of this subject to which we could refer clients. Not surprisingly, most of what is available is on the web. Here are some links that supplement the information provided here:

- **http://wdvl.com/Internet/Management/.** The *Web Developer's Virtual Library* is an excellent general resource for anyone wanting to know more in the way of technical details about web authoring, website management, and so on. This article by Charlie Morris is titled "There's Gold in Them There Log Files!" and is the best general overview of log files and log file applications that I have found, other than the one currently in your hands. It contains information of interest to developers, such as working JavaScript code examples, that goes beyond the information presented in this chapter.
- **http://www.apacheweek.com/.** This site has a lot of information about this very popular, open-source web server. It contains useful discussions of topics such as HTTP and referrer logs that are applicable in a general way to other web servers.
- **http://www.ncsa.uiuc.edu/.** NCSA, as many of you know, was the home of Mosaic, the browser that started all the World Wide Web excitement. If you

do a search on "log files" here, you will uncover a number of good basic articles on log file analysis. One article in particular, "In Search of the Elusive User: Gathering Information on Web Server Access," by Joel Riphagen and Alaina Kanfer, Ph.D. (October 14, 1996: **http://www.ncsa.uiuc.edu/edu/trg/ webstats/index-r.html**), is a very good introduction that goes into more technical detail than I do here. Unfortunately, the article is somewhat dated. The information about particular web analysis products is so badly dated as to be useless. The same is true, sadly, for the references at the end of the article. (Thus we have an interesting illustration of the problems associated with using the web as a research archive.)

- **http://www.w3.org/Daemon/User/Config/Logging.html.** This link provides a brief technical description of the Common Log File format as recommended by the World Wide Web Consortium (W3C), the group that recommends what is in HTML, HTTP, and so on.

There is also, almost certainly, technical documentation that describes various log file options that come with your web server software. In general, with the exception of the Apache server reference noted earlier, such documentation is focused on telling your technical staff *how* to enable and turn off different options rather than *why* you should care about the options or what you might do with the data. It is probably not of much interest to you unless you are interested in technical details.

If you have purchased a log file analysis tool, it, too, comes with documentation that talks about log file analysis. Again, the focus is typically more on *how* than on *why*. Depending on your level of technical interest in just how your particular log file analysis tool works and what it can do, you may find this documentation useful. The companies providing log file analysis software also sometimes provide short courses in the use of their tools. The courses of this kind that I have attended have been useful but, understandably, focus more on how to use the product than on the more general questions of how to integrate the use with the goals of your web business.

CHAPTER THREE

Answering the Basic Questions

Objectives of This Chapter

- Identify four key questions that you should be able to answer about your web business.
- Show how you can use the knowledge from Chapter 2, about the contents of log files, to answer these four key questions.

Putting Log File Analysis to Use

In the preceding chapter, we identified four basic questions that any web business should be able to answer:

1. How much use is the website getting?
2. What parts of the site get the most use? What is it that visitors are interested in?
3. How do people find out about the site? Where are they coming from?
4. Is the site functional in terms of the intended purpose? Are people using it as we would expect them to?

After listing the questions, we turned our attention to the log files themselves, which provide the information needed to answer these questions. With the log file information in hand, we can now return to our basic questions.

I have found that companies are often overwhelmed by even simple questions. A short time ago, I was working with a company that sells industrial supplies. In looking at its web business plans, I became quite concerned about the possibility that the company's web catalog might actually hurt business, which is currently sustaining fairly high margins on equipment. In particular, I was worried that visitors might use the web catalog to do equipment selection but then, having identified just what part they needed, shop elsewhere to find a lower price. It occurred to me that we could use some of the offers currently on the company's website to set up an experiment to find out whether there was any substance to my concerns.

The client responded with surprising exasperation. The project manager came very close to suggesting that I must be sadly naïve to think that the company could use data from its website to run experiments and to look at such detailed business questions. He went on to tell me that the site was not a toy site, had too many visitors, and generated far too much data to enable the company to really use the data for much. In his mind, apparently, being an active web business with an active site moves the company beyond being able to use the website data to understand the business.

This is an unusually candid expression of a viewpoint that is shared by a great many businesses. In conversations with many other business managers, I have had people tell me that they feel that they are doing well to get just the top-level results from their website data within a week of its collection. Yes, websites can generate a lot of data, and, yes, sorting through all the data for general insights can be an overwhelming task. The key is in asking a few focused questions. If you know what questions are important, then, more often than not, log file analysis can help produce the answers.

Focusing on Key Questions

One very common mistake that companies make as they approach analysis of data collected on their websites is that they view log files as something to be "mined." They collect a lot of data over a period of time and let it pile up, with the idea that someday they will dig through it to find the nuggets of business insight that are buried inside.

The problem with this approach is that, without an advance plan to direct the analysis, the nuggets of insight are not usually worth the time and effort spent in the digging. There are a couple of reasons for this. One is that log file data is diffuse. The valuable stuff is distributed more like dust than like nuggets. This makes it difficult to find much of interest without refining the data, analyzing it, and assembling it into a bigger picture. Setting up the "refinery" requires having a good idea of what you want to come out of the back end of the process.

Another problem with the digging-through-the-data approach is that the key to efficient analysis is to throw away the data that you don't need. But you can't very well start throwing data away unless you know in advance what you want to keep.

In the face of such problems, it is not surprising that the most successful approaches to web business analysis typically begin by identifying the key questions that need to be answered. The four questions listed at the beginning of this chapter are a good starting point. Let's look at each of them in detail. As you will see, each of these questions reaches surprisingly deep into your business.

How Much Use Is the Website Getting?

This question is probably the most basic one of all. If nobody is coming to look at your site, what is the point? Yet many businesses have only a vague and often incorrect idea of how many visitors their sites get. Just as bad, they have no idea whether the traffic ebbs and flows in response to company mailings, advertising, and announcements. Without a basic idea of how much traffic you are getting and of what affects the traffic, it is hard to have anything at all to say about a web business.

It does not follow that there is any single right answer about the *amount* of traffic that a site should have. In particular, it is not always true that more is better. It all depends on what you are wanting to do with the site.

I know, for example, of a market research company that uses its website to deliver research reports to its paying subscribers. Although new, potential subscribers can visit the site to look at sample reports, the web is not critical to actually finding the new prospects. Instead, the company identifies and calls on new subscribers through a direct sales organization. For this company, the right number of visitors is scaled directly to its subscriber base. The company *does* want to see a lot of use by these subscribers. It would not expect growth of traffic that was not connected to growth of the subscriber base, however.

On the other hand, I know of another company that sells marine equipment over the web. Revenues come directly from web transactions. For this company, increases in traffic are direct measures of success. More is definitely better.

All of which is to say that even something as seemingly straightforward as measuring traffic must be informed by a clear model of your web business: Just what are you trying to do on the web? It is the answer to this question that will lead to understanding how much traffic you expect to see when the business is working well.

In any case, however, you need to have a good measure of the amount of site activity. When measuring traffic through the use of log files, you should keep in mind the limitations and difficulties that can be associated with log file analysis:

- **Units of counting.** Define a meaningful measure other than the sheer count of the number of requests reaching your sever. As we saw in Chapter 2, the number of hits (requests) is not the same as the number of actual page views. Later, in Chapter 4, we will look at how to collect page views into "visits." For some businesses, visits may be an even better unit of counting than page views.
- **Spurious traffic.** Be sure to filter out visits from your own staff, from web crawlers, and from sources other than the visitors in whom you are interested.
- **Timeliness.** Make sure that you are collecting and distributing this information on a timely basis. When you are in the midst of an ad campaign, for example, it is much more useful to be able to see the effects of the campaign immediately rather than after two months. Changes and trends are often more informative than absolute counts.

What Parts of the Site Get the Most Use?

Think back to the CPS story in Chapter 1. CPS set out to use the web as a new sales channel for its software products. It hoped, as well, to develop a good set of prospects for its services business. Product sales did not increase, however, and new customers for the services business did not materialize. At first, it looked as though the problem were related to our first question about overall visitor volume: There simply were not enough visitors. But then, as traffic increased, product and services sales still did not materialize.

The explanation of the problem emerged as CPS began looking in more detail at just which parts of the site people were visiting. Almost all of the activity was in the free-download area of the site. Practically speaking, nobody ever looked at CPS's descriptions of the products and services that were at the heart of the business. The somewhat shocking realization was that although CPS thought of itself as a highly skilled, specialized solutions company, the visitors on the web had decided that the company was a free software outfit. The web had found a purpose for CPS that was not at all aligned with what CPS needed to do to survive and grow.

CPS didn't need to do focus interviews or anything else very complicated to get this piece of market intelligence. All that was needed was to begin paying attention to which pages were getting the bulk of the traffic on the website and which pages were rarely visited.

To get a different but complementary perspective on site usage, consider the task facing news organizations such as the *New York Times* and the BBC. They have many different kinds of content for their sites. Which ones are readers most interested in? Where should these organizations invest their resources as they focus and develop their sites? What parts of the sites account for the bulk of the traffic at different times of day?

Log file analysis, unassisted by more complicated, specialized techniques, is able to provide this kind of information. As in the case of collecting overall traffic information, you need to be sensitive to the limitations and difficulties associated with log file analysis: You must define a useful unit for counting, filter out certain traffic, and plan through the complications of dealing with a lot of data on busy sites.

How Do People Find Out about the Site?

Most sites want to build traffic. This leads naturally to the question of where visitors come from. Referrer information in log files can help answer this question. Moreover, in studying these results, you can begin to answer a couple of other important questions. The first is "What kinds of visitors did we expect to get who aren't showing up?" The second is "Which promotions and other attempts to drive traffic work, and which don't?"

There is, necessarily, a background question that needs to be coupled with any thinking about visitor traffic, and that is "What techniques are you using to increase traffic?" Let's discuss the alternatives.

Some of the most obvious approaches to building traffic on your website rely on getting visibility on other websites. Advertising is the most obvious way to do this, but smaller companies usually find that buying advertising space on the web is pretty expensive. Bigger companies can probably afford the expense but might reasonably ask about the effectiveness of the advertising spending. It is often more productive and economical to drive traffic by working collaboratively with other sites that can link back to your site. These relationships can take dozens of different forms. In CPS's case, we saw that the company was able to drive traffic by notifying other sites that it was offering software tools for free. (We also note that CPS had some trouble converting these visitors into buyers—perhaps because there was no direct upgrade path from the free product to the licensed product.)

Coverage in industry news stories is another way to drive traffic. You can also write articles that are published on other sites. These articles typically focus on issues, trends, and new developments in your industry rather than just on your own product or service. In return for the articles, you get links back to your site. Moderating industry discussion groups on trade sites is yet another way to drive traffic.

Each of these relationships with other sites can be evaluated in terms of effectiveness. Because most of the traffic from such promotions will arrive through links from the other sites, referrer entries in the log file can give you a very direct picture of how much traffic is due to each link. You will also want to keep an eye out for spikes in general traffic levels that are tied to the release of an article on another site. Do keep in mind that, even in the case of articles and links placed on other sites, you are building general visibility and brand awareness while you are providing links. It is possible that some people will not follow a link immediately but will remember your company's name and come to the site at some later time by entering your primary URL.

Another source of traffic is links from search engines on portal sites. Many companies starting out with a web business assume that this will be a significant source of traffic. Sometimes, this is true, particularly if the website is offering information or services that are somewhat unique (e.g., "giant schnauzer rescue"). On the other hand, if you are offering "ERP system integration services," the odds of your getting much traffic through search terms are actually quite small. Still, you will almost surely get some, and you should know which words are working for you. You can then make sure that these terms are included in the metadata tags for your pages. The terms also show you more about how visitors are using your site. Once again, this kind of information comes directly out of analysis of referrer record information in the log file.

Internet links, search engines, and advertising are not necessarily the most effective ways to drive traffic. Many companies find that it is activity outside the Internet, such as trade shows, promotional mailings, and articles in print magazines, that is most effective in increasing company visibility and site traffic. Measuring the effectiveness of such non-web promotions is more difficult because you cannot simply look at the referrer log. One obvious approach to measuring the effectiveness of shows and other promotions is by paying attention to timing, looking for increases in traffic shortly after the event. Clearly, this technique can give you only an approximation of effectiveness. A more direct approach depends on setting up some other entry points into your site, with different URLs. (They can simply be copies of your home page that are on different parts of your site.) Your promotional information, whether it is show literature, mailings, or even business cards, can use the different URLs so that you can get a better idea of which traffic is coming from which kind of promotional activity. This, again, is information that is very easy to get from a log file: You simply compare the levels of activity for the different entry pages.

Is the Site Functioning as Expected?

This question is often a very difficult one because many companies do not carefully articulate their expectations before getting into the web business. In interviews with scores of companies, we often find that there are multiple, and usually unstated, expectations from different parts of the organization. For example, in talking to one large entertainment company with interests in films, television, and music, we learned that upper management viewed the website as a promotional expense not significantly different from, say, newspaper and magazine advertising. People closer to the web business had a more web-specific view of the site's function that was tied to a notion of wanting to build a "web community." Unfortunately, in addition to being out of sync with corporate management, they had no particularly well-formed notion of how to make money from a web community: Sell some advertising maybe? Sell T-shirts? Given the breadth and vagueness of these objectives, it was tough to know what success looked like, much less whether the company was achieving it.

Discussions about whether the company should invest more in its web presence became a tangled mix of discussions about corporate objectives and concerns about site performance, as if site performance was an objective in itself. What kind of performance? For what end? The lack of a clear, broadly agreed-upon model of the purpose and function of the web business made it difficult for this company to see that business outcomes and website performance are separate concerns that should be connected through measurement and analysis.

This company is not unusual. Companies that are pure web plays typically know why they have a website since it *is* the business. But for established companies with revenues that are only tangentially related to the web, the answer to the question, "So why are you bothering to be on the web? What's the point?" is often, "Well, we simply must have a web presence." I say, probably so, but *why?*

The problem with not having clearly stated expectations for the way that the website will contribute to the business is that it is impossible to know whether the website is succeeding. It is not enough simply to know that you have a couple of thousand visits a day and that the traffic is increasing. Remember that CPS managed to increase traffic without providing the benefit that it needed for its business.

What is the benefit that your website is supposed to create for your business? Being able to answer this question, write the answer down, and get agreement about the answer within your organization is a prerequisite to knowing whether your website is performing as it should.

Given a statement of the high-level goals for the website, it is possible to use log files to raise interesting questions about how the website should be changed to better meet these goals. For example, consider the case of one web company that sells news and entertainment publications. In addition to building the site and offering the publications for sale, the company has made a considerable investment in creating original stories about the publications that it sells. The website is constructed to focus on these stories as a primary selling tool. As you browse through the site, the original writing by the company's own staff makes for interesting, fast reading that provides a snapshot of how the media are covering the most current news and entertainment. One of the objectives for this website, clearly articulated by management and built into the structure of the company, is to create interest in the publications that will lead to sales.

The surprising news from the site's log files, however, was that a quarter of the visitors simply use the site's online search tool to go directly to a particular publication and bypass the news and opinion pieces. The fact that a substantial number of visitors were skipping around the content created by the company's staff suggested that the company should learn more about how the content was being used. The next step, which is still in process, is to do a more careful analysis to see which visitors are doing most of the buying and to see how return visitors use the site and make purchases. Taken far enough, the company should be able to build a model that shows how its customers are segmented between one-time buyers and returning customers, readers and goal-oriented search-engine users, buyers and lookers.

This story is a good illustration of using log files coupled with a list of basic questions to get insight about a business. This company did take the time to articulate a model of how it expected the website to work. With the model in hand, it was easy to use simple, readily available log file data to address the question, Is the site functioning as we expect? The answer was maybe. But maybe not. The log file analysis, as is often the case, did not provide a black-and-white, yes-or-no answer.

Instead, it served as an "indicator" (like a warning light on a dashboard) pointing to something that deserves closer scrutiny. Getting the more detailed answers requires access to information beyond the scope of simple log files, including registration information (to look at return users) and purchase data. But the log files by themselves were able to show that the matter deserves looking at. This is exactly right. Because log files are large and expensive to analyze in detail, they are most useful as a way to make sure that everything is working according to your expectations and objectives. When the log file analysis turns up something that doesn't quite fit with expectations, then it is time to take on the expense of digging more deeply.

Summary

There are a handful of very important questions that you need to answer once you start looking seriously at the performance of your web business. The good news is that most of these questions can be answered directly from log file analysis.

The first key question involves the volume of log file activity and how that volume changes over time. We note that interpreting the answers to even this most straightforward of questions involves having some kind of model of what your web business is all about. More traffic is not necessarily a good thing if it is not the right kind of traffic.

The idea of the "right kind" of traffic leads to the second key question, which revolves around what people actually do once they are on the site. Understanding which parts of the site get the most use is critical not only to knowing what is working and what isn't but also to understanding how the Internet community values and uses your web business.

The third critical question is how people find out about your site, which generally translates into how you can go about getting more of the right kind of visitors. There are a number of ways to build relationships with other sites that can lead users to your site; you can measure the success of these techniques by looking at the information collected in the referrer records in your log files. Referrer records are also useful for understanding which search terms bring people to your site. In evaluating the effectiveness of non-web promotions in driving traffic, it is often possible to get at least approximate measures of effectiveness by using different URL entry points to the site in the different promotions.

The fourth and most difficult of the key questions is whether your site is performing as expected. The question is difficult because it presumes that you can articulate your expectations. We find that most companies have at least some difficulty in doing this in a way that consolidates the viewpoints of different stake-holders in the business and that is concise enough to lead to specific, measurable performance expectations. Despite the difficulty, it is critical to formulate such performance expectations. One obvious benefit is that the company will perform more effectively if everybody is sharing the same goals and vision. Another more prosaic but also very important benefit is that clearly formulated expectations allow you to use log file analysis as a set of "indicator lights" that allow you to quickly and inexpensively check to see whether the business is working as you expect it to. When simple log file analysis shows that there is deviation from the expectations, setting off a warning light, then it is possible to dig more deeply, beyond the log file measures, to try to understand what is really happening.

Key Ideas

- You must approach website data analysis with a clear notion of what you want to find. It is usually easiest to frame this notion in terms of key questions. The key questions become the foundation of your data analysis effort.
- One of your key tasks is to formulate a clear written statement of what should be happening on the website, assuming that the business model works as planned.
- The goal of an effective website analysis program is to monitor deviations from the expected behavior of the business. Set up a system that gives you a warning light when something is not operating as expected within the business model.

CHAPTER FOUR

Getting More from Website Data

Objectives of This Chapter

- Explain why the idea of keeping track of visits rather than just page views is important.
- Provide ways to extract visits from log file data, giving you a sense of why doing this is somewhat arbitrary.
- Provide insight into some of the practical operational considerations in analyzing log files on sites where there is a lot of traffic.

Visits

When you are running a web business, you want more visitors. Just as important, you want the visitors to come back. Ideally, the effect of a first visit is that people bookmark your site. Over a series of visits, you want these *visitors* to become *customers.* Once they are customers, you want to ensure that each subsequent visit is satisfying and meets their expectations so that they keep coming back.

In short, you want each visit, from the first one onward, to be a positive experience. You want the visits to build up and change over time so that the customer really becomes *your* customer. The web, as is often said but less often practiced, is about engaging the customer and creating relationships. Central to this engagement is a focus on the "visit" and on making each visit count.

Thinking about visits is easier if we get away from the web for a moment and consider a more concrete example of visits. Suppose we are running a coffee shop (which is not that far from running a web business, after all). Because we are focused on drawing more traffic to our shop in a very competitive market, we want to understand more about why people come to our coffee shop. The fact that we serve good coffee is part of the answer, of course, but most of the competing coffee shops offer that, too. So, as we get to thinking about what makes our business work, we come up with questions. Does the amount of time spent waiting in line matter? Might we make more money if we bought a second cappuccino machine and staffed for a second *barista*, thus reducing the waiting time? Does the availability of open seating have an impact on the amount of coffee sold? Do people buy more coffee as they stay longer? Or do they just occupy a seat without producing revenue? Maybe we would make more money if we reduced the amount of seating and moved people through the shop more quickly. On the other hand, does the ability to sit, and not buy coffee, draw people back again and again, thus producing more revenue over time? Maybe the seating is part of why people come to buy our coffee rather than going to the competitor down the street.

From the perspective of a web business, the great thing about a coffee shop is that you can look out from behind the counter, count the number of people at tables, and see what is going on. Over time, you can watch the duration of visits and keep track of what is sold to the people in the shop if they sit down with a book and stay for an hour or so. You can keep track of return customers, noting whether the regular customers are the ones who sit for a while or the ones who dash in and out. You can, in short, get a feel for the business just by paying attention.

What you are paying attention to in the coffee shop goes beyond the individual cup of coffee that you serve. It is focused on understanding "visits" to the coffee shop. The questions we are asking have to do with the revenue produced in a visit, the duration of visits, what people do during a visit, and the likelihood of return visits. The goal is to sell more cups of coffee, but understanding how to reach this goal requires grouping the individual transactions into the broader notion of a visit.

It is important to note that, even in the relatively concrete context of a coffee shop, visits are something of an artificial construct. If I come in for coffee in the morning and then again in the afternoon, that almost certainly counts as two visits. But what if I go out and come back twice in the same morning? What if I just go out to feed the parking meter and then come back? What if the time that I spend away from the coffee shop stretches to half an hour?

Two important points emerge from these questions. The first is that the notion of a visit involves some kind of definition of continuous activity, interrupted by only relatively short time intervals. The second is that the definition is arbitrary and can vary from observer to observer (and, in the case of computerized systems, from system to system).

Let's change our coffee shop setup so that it is a little bit more like a website. Suppose that you have to figure out how the coffee shop was working without being able to scan the tables. Suppose that the only data you can get is from a log sheet that is maintained by an assistant. Thinking through what needs to be on this log sheet will help us in understanding how to make use of website log file data as we reconstruct website visits.

Suppose that the coffee log records only the time of day when each cup is served, along with what was served. This is analogous to the log file information that tells us when each page is served. We would be able to answer the sorts of general questions we looked at in Chapter 3. We would have a good idea of overall volume and of how it changes over the course of the day. We would also know how many "hits" were for house coffee as opposed to espresso drinks and could look at questions about transaction volume and value. But—and this is important—we wouldn't be able to tell anything about visits at all since there would be no way to tie transactions together. All we would have is transactions, unrelated to individual customers.

We could improve the recording system by giving each person a numbered coffee cup as he or she came in the door. Our coffee service log could then record not only the time that each cup was served but also the number of the cup. If the log showed that cup 16 was used for a cappuccino at 9:20 A.M., and then for another cappuccino at 9:35, then, for a cup of coffee at 9:48 and a cup of coffee at 10:10, we would have pretty good reason to believe that someone visited the shop between 9:20 and 10:10 and made four purchases. (We would also be pretty sure that the person was wired when he or she left.)

But what if cup 23 was used for a cup of coffee at 8:53 A.M. and then for a cup of coffee at 10:17? What if we know that the staff regularly busses the tables, places the cups in a dishwasher, and washes a load of cups at least once every hour? Obviously, someone could have bought a cup of coffee, sat down with a good book in a comfortable chair, and then bought a second cup a little over an hour later. Or it could have been two different people and two visits. We might arbitrarily decide that if more than an hour passes between transactions for any particular cup, we would treat the two purchases as originating from two visits, but we wouldn't know for sure.

Thinking about the coffee shop problem is useful because it suggests strategies for reconstructing visits on a website. The log and numbered cups system is reasonably analogous to the situation we face when trying to construct visits from a log file just by using IP addresses. If there is a lot of activity associated with the same IP address, we are often safe in assuming that it is connected to a single visit. But, as intervals between page requests increase to, say, 15 minutes or half an hour, it is less and less likely that it constitutes a visit. Sure, it is possible that someone is visiting the site, takes a phone call, and then continues his or her visit. That probably happens often. It is also likely that we are dealing with a different visitor and a different visit.

Actually, our situation as web business managers is more difficult than that of the coffee shop owner in one important respect. To make the numbered cup system fully analogous to the use of IP addresses, we would also have to introduce large batches of cups that all share the same number. This is obviously a bad idea since it will create confusion. It is also exactly what happens when we have multiple visitors from a service like AOL or a big company like IBM, all of whom might share the same IP address as they visit the site. So, let's begin our discussion about visits to websites (rather than coffee shops) by looking more closely at IP addresses.

The Visitor's IP Address

Consider our visitor from IP address 207.94.105.77—the one who we followed through the different pages of the sample website in Chapter 2. How much do we know about this person? The referrer log tells us that he or she came to the site from the *KM World* site. If we assume that this IP address belongs to the same person over the few minutes that it took to make the page requests that we tracked in Chapter 2, we know something about what the visitor did and looked at. But can we tell whether this is someone who has visited the site before? Would we be able to recognize this person if he or she comes back? (This is an important question because if we can recognize someone over a series of visits, then we can put together a richer picture of the person's interests than we can from a single visit. We can also begin to answer important questions about things such as the pattern of activities, over time, that leads up to a purchase.)

The logical place to start with this inquiry is with the IP address itself. Does the actual address tell us anything?

In this instance, the IP address belongs to Netcom, an Internet service provider (ISP) located in San Jose, California. So it could be that this visitor is someone located in California. But maybe not. Netcom (recently acquired by Mindspring) serves a national customer base. The Internet, after all, is a world-wide network.

So, in this case at least, the IP address is not very informative. Sadly, from the perspective of companies wanting to know more about the visitors to their sites, this relatively low level of information available from the IP address tends to be the norm rather than the exception. For most companies looking at the IP addresses of visitors to their websites, the addresses typically fall into four categories, as described in Table 4–1.

As you can see from even a cursory glance at this table, there are very few instances in which an IP address tells you very much. Even the general *domain* (e.g., .com, .ca, .de) of the address can be misleading. It is a reasonably safe bet that someone coming from an address with the domain of .ca is from Canada and that someone from .de is from Germany, but assuming that the domain of .com is evidence that the visitor is from a U.S. company is just a good guess: It is more likely true than not, but far from certain.

The bottom line, then, is that IP addresses are a long way from being like a Social Security number or DNA sample; they almost never point to a particular individual. Worse than being anonymous, they are not even unique in any important sense:

- It is not possible to assume that an IP address is uniquely associated with just one person at any given time. Several different visitors coming from behind a firewall may share the same address. If a lot of this is happening at once, it can be difficult to simply disentangle one visitor from another.
- It is very difficult to know if and when a visitor returns. This is obviously true for visitors coming from behind a firewall since we can't identify them uniquely even during the initial visit, but it is also true for visitors with dynamically assigned IP addresses since those addresses are not constant from visit to visit.

This situation is worse for consumer sites than for business-to-business sites since proportionately more of the visitors will be from service providers like Netcom and from online communities such as AOL. With the business sites, you

**Table 4–1 Different Kinds of Visitors and What You Can Learn
                  about Them**

Kind of Visitor	Good News/Bad News
Subscriber to a large service, such as AOL, that provides services from behind a firewall	Practically speaking, these visitors are anonymous. Visitors from services such as AOL reach your site from behind a firewall that screens the identity of the individual users and hookups. Consequently, many different individuals reaching your site from AOL will all share the same IP address, *all at the same time.* It is thus impossible to even tell one user from another on the basis of an IP address, much less know much about individual visitors. Consumer sites report having up to 80 percent of their visitors from AOL, all using a few AOL addresses that aggregate and blur together many users at once.
Subscriber to an Internet service provider (ISP) that assigns IP addresses dynamically	These visitors are more distinct. Unlike the AOL scenario, where many users will share a single IP address at the same time, these visitors will typically have a unique IP address for the duration of each visit. But, because the IP addresses are assigned to the ISP's customers dynamically as they log onto the system, the same visitor will typically have a different IP address from visit to visit. One nice thing: You can sometimes have some success in at least identifying the general area of the country where these visitors come from. For example, if you have a visitor coming in from an IP address assigned to GWI.NET, which serves most of Maine, it is a pretty good bet that the visitor has some association with Maine.

Kind of Visitor	Good News/Bad News
Employee of a large company	These visitors look a lot like the folks from service providers such as AOL. It might be interesting, for example, to know that someone associated with IBM is visiting your site, but that doesn't really tell you much. Like visitors from AOL, the visitor from IBM or some other big company is typically coming from behind a firewall, which means that many visitors will all have the same address even if they are on your site at the same time.
Employee of a small company	These are probably the most uniquely defined visitors to your site. If your competitors are small companies, it should be easy to know when they are looking at your site if they use their corporate Internet access. As in the other instances, you typically cannot tell one individual from another.

might at least know that people from XYZ company are coming to your site a lot, even if you cannot identify them as individuals. But, overall, it is clear that the IP address information in the log file records provides very little insight into who is visiting the site at an individual level.

Pulling In Other Information

The fact that IP addresses are not tightly coupled to individual visitors makes it difficult to even reconstruct a single visit with certainty, much less recognize people over time, from visit to visit. We know that understanding how people use a website, just like understanding how people use a coffee shop, depends on understanding what happens during a typical visit. So it is pretty clear that we need to find some other kinds of information that will allow us to do a better job of recognizing individuals and of collecting information about visits.

Referrer Information Used to Reconstruct a Visit

First, let's rule out an approach that seems logical at first but doesn't work in practice. This will save you from even considering it.

A visit is a sequence of page requests, so reconstructing a visit is really an attempt to string together such a sequence. We learned in Chapter 2 that referrer information allows us to know the URL of the previous page when a visitor has followed a link to reach the current page. So referrer entries should be useful in reconstructing the sequence of requests that comprise a visit, right?

Although this is true in principle, there are some limitations that keep it from being true in practice, particularly on busy sites. The primary difficulty is that reconstructing literal "chains" of visits takes a great deal of computation. For sites with heavy traffic, running into the range of hundreds of thousands to millions of visits a day, the processing burden of doing even the most basic log file analysis is substantial. Trying to thread together all the sequences of referrer log entries is simply too expensive.

Referrer entries are useful for discovering where people are coming from to reach your site, learning which pages are typically the entry pages, uncovering the search terms used to reach your site, and seeing whether there are surprising "exit" pages—the last pages viewed before leaving your site. But using them to reconstruct whole sequences, to solve the "visit" problem, is more trouble than it is worth.

Other Approaches to Constructing Visits from Log Files

There are other tricks that log file analysis tools use to help you do a better job of reconstructing visits. They typically involve collecting other information about the visitor and then tying it to the IP address. The combination is more likely to be unique than is either piece of information standing by itself.

For example, the log file analysis tool can note the make and version of the browser that the visitor is using and can add this information to the IP address to create a stronger identifier. Going back to our coffee shop example, it would be like noting the color of the buyer's shirt in addition to the number of the coffee cup. So in trying to decide whether the purchases at 8:53 A.M. and 10:17 A.M. constituted one visit or two, we could check to see whether the shirt color was the same. On the website, we look at the IP address *and* the make and version of the browser. There is certainly more than one customer with a blue shirt, just as there is more than one visitor using Netscape 4.06. All the same, extra information can sometimes help.

Use of Cookies

If you were a consultant hired to help us analyze activity in our coffee shop, you would very probably be amazed by the numbered cups and notes about shirt color. You might observe that our primary problem is that our numbered cups and other records failed to uniquely tie a transaction to a particular buyer. And, you would surely note that, for all of our record keeping, we still had no way to learn about return visits. The problem, you would note, is that there is no long-term relationship between a buyer and a cup number. Without some way to recognize returning customers, the shop would not be able to answer critically important questions about what makes people come back to buy coffee day after day.

Not surprisingly, all our attempts to use referrer logs, browser identities, and other hints in the log file leave us in exactly the same spot as we would be with our coffee shop. Nothing we have talked about so far helps us know whether people are coming back.

Understanding this limitation puts you in the position to understand why websites are so fond of "cookies." Suppose, instead of numbering the cups in the coffee shop, we provided customers with a little card that they would use each time they made a purchase. We could use the number on the card as a key into a database where we kept track of the time and date of purchases. By analyzing the information in the database, we could come up with a picture of customer behavior, over time, across visits, that is much more accurate and complete than the inferential conclusions drawn from our numbered cup log.

Cookies, which are small bits identifying information that are stored on the computer used to run the web browser, are the functional equivalent of the plastic ID card. Someone else might be using the computer containing the cookie from time to time, just as someone might borrow someone else's card. The cards and cookies, however, are a big step toward keeping track of customers from visit to visit.

Our coffee shop example is also useful in that it brings a couple of interesting issues surrounding cookies into sharp perspective. Why would customers ever bother to carry a plastic card and present it when purchasing coffee? The answer is that they wouldn't unless it provided them with some advantage that they cared about. Consequently, retail stores like Safeway that use ID cards as keys into

databases offer an inducement to using the cards. The most common inducement is that the buyer pays less. We might charge 25 cents less for a cup of coffee
for members of our "Coffee Club," and the card would be the buyer's way of
showing that he or she is a member.

Two things stand out in this example. The first is that the buyer knows that
he or she is using the card. The second is that he or she gets something in return.
Interestingly, in this regard, cookies do not work the same way as the membership card. Unlike someone fishing a card out of his or her wallet, people receiving
cookies typically don't know that they are doing so. They often get no obvious
benefit in return. This can be a problem, just as it would be if there were no dis-
count associated with the card. We will explore these issues in depth later when
we look in detail at the use of cookies.

For now, the key point is that cookies do provide a reasonably reliable way to
recognize returning visitors. They are therefore an important, useful tool for
reconstructing visits so that we can evaluate the quality of visits and look at what
keeps people coming back. As you may remember from Chapter 2, cookie information can be stored in log files and can therefore become part of the log file
analysis process.

Registration

As useful as cookies are, they, too, can produce confused identities any time that
more than one person uses a computer. The problem is that the cookie is associated with the computer, not with the person. So the most reliable way to obtain
the identities of visitors is to ask them. Clearly, even this is not foolproof since
people can provide false identities. Even a false identity is probably consistent from
visit to visit, however, and so gives us what we need in order to analyze what happens during and between visits.

Registration information is typically coupled with cookies. The reason, which
we will explore in more detail in Chapter 6 on cookies, is that, once a visitor has
"signed in" with his or her name and password, the cookie provides a way to tie
together all the activities during the visit. (Clearly, visitors would not want to provide a name and password for every page. Cookies keep that from happening.)

Getting people to provide identifying information can be difficult. It requires,
even more than cookies, that you provide them with something in return. This is
an issue that we will explore in much more detail in later chapters, as we look at
providing visitors with personalized web pages and with other information that is
tailored to their needs.

Operational Considerations

Overview of the Log File Analysis Process

At this point, we have taken a close look at where log files come from, what they contain, and how this information is expressed inside the log file. We have also considered what you can, at least in principle, do with log files. Now let's move from principle to practice: What steps are involved in turning a log file into a useful view of website activity? How much time and effort are required? What kinds of problems do companies typically encounter?

Figure 4–1 illustrates the steps in a typical log file processing operation for sites using more than a single web server. If there is only one web server, the collect and merge steps drop out of the picture, and the log file goes directly into the filter and load operation.

The *collect* step in this sequence is simple if all of the web servers are in one physical location. Some large active sites use web servers that are distributed geographically, however, sometimes on different continents, to improve performance. Log files, you will remember, are large. Even when compressed, a day's log

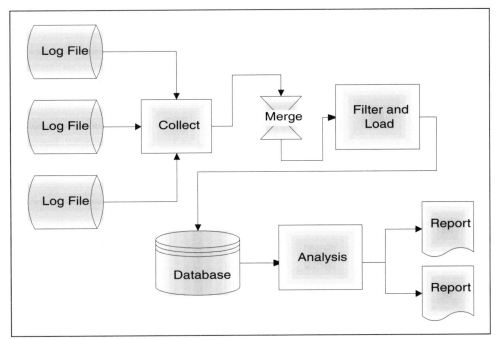

Figure 4–1 Steps in processing log files

file from a very active site can reach almost a gigabyte in size. Transmitting log files to a central collecting place for further processing can take time.

Once the files are brought together into a single physical location, they need to be *merged* to create a single overall view of the site's activity. The requirement for the merge step becomes immediately obvious when you consider what happens on a site with load-balanced servers, a commonly used arrangement where each request goes to the server that, at that instant, is least busy and therefore best able to handle the request. The result is that the requests from any particular user during any particular visit are probably scattered across the log files from different servers. Reconstructing the visit can happen only after the different transactions constituting the visit are reassembled into a single sequence.

The merging process (some vendors of site analysis tools refer to it as "stitching" or "sewing") can be quite time-consuming. The reason for this isn't surprising. The process has to operate on the log files in full, expanded form. Just the sheer amount of data movement involved in reading through gigabytes of data, merging it, and outputting it again takes time. Companies with large, active sites can spend hours each night just running the merge process.

Once the log files have been merged, they are imported into a database for analysis. (In practice, the merging and importing might be handled by a single process to reduce I/O costs, but it is useful, in any case, to think of them as separate operations even if they do just stream from one to the other.) This import process involves at least two important operations: *filtering* the records to focus only on useful information and *loading* the records into the database by transforming the human-readable text into binary fields and records.

The filtering step is important because, as we have seen, much of the information in a log file is not particularly useful in the analysis process. The filter process, for example, typically screens out log file entries that are simply calls for style sheets or calls for graphic elements such as bullets and logos. There is no

---

Technical Note: Merging

This merging process is one area where network sniffers, which we mentioned briefly in Chapter 2, can really make a difference. If the sniffer is placed in the right location on your network, it will intercept all the traffic from all the web servers, obviating the need for any stitching.

reason to place such information in the database. It will not contribute to the analysis but will, instead, only slow the analysis process down by adding to the size of the database. Companies may also filter out records from particular IP addresses. Typically, for example, you are not interested in including transactions from your own staff in the visitor data that you want to analyze. The more you can pare the data down without losing any valuable information, the faster will be the subsequent log file analysis.

Different log file analysis products use different approaches to organizing the underlying stored data. Some use relational databases, others use data warehouses on top of databases, and some use object databases. The differences in the underlying data representation, coupled with different implementation approaches, mean that the products perform differently when there are enormous amounts of data that must be loaded and analyzed. For sites with heavy traffic, it is possible for the filtering and loading process to take three or four hours.

Once the raw log file data has been filtered, digested, and converted into database records, you are ready to begin the analysis of the data so that you can generate reports. The cost of the analysis, measured in time, varies with the nature of the questions that you are asking. Simple frequency information, such as counts of visits or information on the pages that are visited most frequently may be available very quickly. Some analysis tools aggregate such information as they load the database, making the answers almost instant. Other, more complicated questions that require joining different kinds of information in the database (for example, questions involving the most common paths through the site or, for visitors primarily interested in sports, the amounts of time spent in other news areas) can be quite time-consuming to answer.

Implications

Here are a few simple pointers to consider as you plan your website analysis program:

- Focus on performance issues when buying log file analysis software. Make sure that the vendor can provide you with customer references of other sites with traffic levels similar to yours. Call those references and ask about the kinds of performance and processing issues that we identify here.
- Recognize that your analysis program needs to be focused on specific questions and designed in advance rather than being an ad hoc "mining" exercise. The data from your website is often simply too voluminous to allow ad hoc

approaches. Instead, you need to start by thinking about your business and, from there, begin to define the questions that you need to answer.

- Keep the number of questions relatively small and focused, digging deeper only when the questions turn up something that is surprising.

Summary

Getting a good understanding of what is happening in your web business requires moving beyond simple frequency counts and basic questions. Central to obtaining a deeper understanding is the notion of a "visit."

Visits are not directly captured in log files or other website data. They must be reconstructed from the data. The reconstruction process necessarily involves making a number of assumptions, such as how much time can pass between page requests before one visit becomes two visits.

Reconstruction of visits is made more complicated by difficulties in accurately identifying individual visitors. The IP address associated with a given visitor at any specific time is, in particular, a very weak indicator of the visitor's identity. The problem in ascertaining identity translates into difficulty in knowing when visitors return.

Cookies provide a mechanism for tying together the activities that constitute a single visit. They can even assist in recognizing visitors as they return to the site. When cookies are coupled with registration information, they become a reasonably reliable tool for studying the activity in individual visits and for understanding which customers return.

The analysis of visit information, along with all other log file analysis, requires that the log files be collected together and processed. Because log files are so large and because they can require significant processing in order to distill out the useful information, it is important to give some careful thought to the selection of log file analysis tools and the design of analysis routines. This is particularly true if you have a heavily used site. It is not unusual for companies to find that their analysis efforts simply take too much time to be timely or worthwhile.

Suggestions for keeping the analysis cost-effective include making sure that the analysis software can scale to meet your needs, aggressively filtering the data as it is loaded into the analysis database, and being parsimonious in your analysis demands. The most important contribution to effective analysis consists of thinking through your business and understanding just what you expect to happen on the website. In that way, the analysis process can focus on signaling you when expectations are not being met and then on supporting you when you dig deeper to understand why.

Key Ideas

- The concept of a "visit" is critical to understanding what is happening in your web business.
- Reconstructing visits is not straightforward. It requires making some assumptions and requires looking at data from a number of sources.
- Cookies are a useful tool in the reconstruction of visits. Particularly when coupled with registration data, cookies help you string together the activities in a single visit and help recognize returning visitors.
- Because log files are big, the processing costs associated with turning log files into something more useful can be substantial. If your site is a busy one, ad hoc analysis is usually out of the question. You should approach log file analysis with a clear idea of what questions you need to answer.

CHAPTER FIVE

Identifying Questions for Your Business Model

Objectives of This Chapter

- Provide a simple, flexible way of thinking about models for web businesses, enabling you to formulate appropriate expectations for your particular business.
- Identify the key questions for each of the different kinds of web businesses. The questions will help you discover whether your expectations are actually being met.
- Show how to separate and keep track of the different functions and goals of your business when you are using a mixed model. Illustrate the dangers inherent in mixed models.
- Provide concrete examples of the different business models, questions, opportunities, and problems so that you can connect the abstractions to the particulars of your business.

We have come a long way from our initial look at CPS and the difficulties that it encountered in becoming a web business. Along the way, we have explored a number of important sources of information about your web business. In particular, we took a close look at log files and other detailed records of what visitors do when they come to your website. These low-level records are the raw material of web business analysis.

We then explored mechanisms for extracting value from these records and identified a few key questions that web businesses should be able to answer, based on the log file data. Then, in the preceding chapter, we introduced the idea of visits, which give you a much more powerful way to look at what is happening in your web business. In subsequent chapters, we will take a close look at cookies, which we already have found to be an important tool for reconstructing visits, and we will then move on to look at how to personalize the site to tighten customer engagement.

Before we head off in new directions, however, we should return to the important matter of identifying the key questions for your business. In addition to the four very general questions that we explored in Chapter 3, there are questions that tie more closely to your particular kind of business. In this chapter, we separate web businesses into a few basic categories and then explore the questions that are most important for each approach to commerce on the web.

Different Kinds of Web Businesses

The Internet has provided fertile soil for the growth of new kinds of businesses. It is literally true that the most interesting approaches to Internet business being developed today were not even visibly on the horizon just a couple of years ago. Any attempt to identify and categorize the different kinds of web businesses is necessarily incomplete.

All the same, the categorization effort is critically important. Businesses with different objectives and revenue models need different kinds of information in order to measure success and monitor progress. It does not make sense to talk about "web business analysis" in general. The analysis needs to be tied to the shape of the business.

The way around the problem of coming up with a workable classification is to keep the classification at a high level. One approach that works well is to "follow the money." In web businesses, money typically comes from one of three places:

1. **Completing sales of goods or services on the web.**
2. **Selling access to web visitors ("eyeballs").** The revenue here is usually from advertising or payment for lead generation. Portals, for example, make their money by providing access to potential customers.
3. **Closing sales of goods or services through non-web channels.** The web is used to support the primary business (e.g., lead generation for a company's own products, customer support for your products, and so on).

These different revenue sources provide a workable framework for categorizing web businesses. Whether you are looking at vertical portals, horizontal portals, infomediaries, net market makers, or any of the other of the dozens of new approaches to web business, the fundamentals of the business model revolve around the sources of revenue.

Each revenue source is coupled with a different set of issues and questions. Making money by providing access to customers, for example, requires a different focus than making money by selling goods. We explore each of these basic web business models in turn in this chapter and conclude by looking at the issues that arise when you try to mix the different kinds of revenue streams.

Closing Sales on the Web

A great many different kinds of companies complete sales of goods or services on the web. This group includes companies as different from one another as small specialty retailers, amazon.com, e-bay, L.L. Bean, and many others on the consumer side. On the business-to-business side, it includes W.W. Grainger, Cisco Systems, National Semiconductor, Chemdex, and many others. It is part of the business model that CPS was trying to execute.

The broad range of these businesses certainly results in a correspondingly broad range of business questions. It is also useful to recognize that, despite all the differences, these businesses share important common requirements and goals. The common goals allow us to come up with a group of questions that apply across all companies working to close business on their websites. As you will see, these questions differ in useful, instructive ways from the questions of interest for other kinds of business, such as those that depend primarily on advertising revenues.

Here is a list of the issues and questions with which businesses selling on the web need to be concerned:

- **Assessing activity.** What are visitors looking for? What do they do while they are on the site?
- **Recognizing buyers and lookers.** How do visitors who become buyers differ from those who don't buy? How can we recognize buyers and serve them better?
- **Turning lookers into buyers.** Is there a way to design the site to funnel visitors into the kinds of activities associated with buying?
- **Making buying easy.** How can you reduce the number of pages that must be viewed to complete a purchase?

- **Having buyers return.** How many buyers are repeat buyers? Is there a repeat-buyer profile? What features do repeat buyers use?

At the simplest level, any company's visitor activity profile emerges from answering the general questions that we looked at in Chapter 3 and that apply to all businesses. When you are using the website to close sales, it is typically worthwhile to look beyond these very basic questions. In particular, you will want to be able to create a map of the primary paths that visitor traffic follows as it flows through the site (e.g., visitors enter at the home page, then go to the list of products, then usually go to the page describing the big widget, and so on). It is easy to construct such maps from log file data by using referrer log entries to keep track of the most frequent page transitions on the site. The process is analogous to looking at footpaths across a grassy field and noting which paths are widest and most worn.

The most critical differences in activity on a site that sells goods and services are the differences between the people who buy and those who just look. Do the site activities show that buyers are a distinctly different group from lookers, apart from the fact of their buying? For example, one business information site that we know of found that visitors linking to the site from the *Wall Street Journal* site were much more likely to buy than those linking from an AOL financial site. This was useful, important information that helped the company be more efficient in its promotional expenditures. A computer equipment site found that people who were making purchases typically knew what they wanted and did not spend a lot of time browsing around on the site. Consequently, the company streamlined its site design, allowing the buyers to get in and out as fast as possible, providing little information to the lookers. A gourmet foods retailer found just the opposite: The best buyers wanted to read about the different foods offered on the site. Consequently, providing rich content and then tying selling to that content became a critical part of site design.

Typically, working with the buyer/looker distinction requires information that goes beyond basic log file record content. In particular, the concept of visits is critical to this kind of inquiry. This means that you will want to be able to keep track of the identity of an individual visitor, even if only anonymously and only for the duration of the visit.

In addition to keeping identities straight, we also need to know who actually bought our goods or services. Better yet, we would like to know how much the person bought and whether he or she is a returning buyer. Answering questions like these requires coordination of the log file activity with a database of infor-mation about particular customers. Cookies are typically the key link for making such connections between log files and databases. The cookie, which can be picked up in one of the fields of the log file record, becomes the index key for tying into the database.

Once you can *distinguish* between buyers and lookers, it is natural to begin thinking about how you can do a better job of *converting* lookers into buyers. It may be that this conversion happens over more than a single visit. Consequently, you will want to think about ways to get at least some of the visitors to register for free information, for free access to a useful service, or for some other attractive offer that allows you to begin to keep track of their visits as they return to the site. Once again, tying into a registration database implies reaching beyond the mere log file records.

The approach to the problem of converting lookers into buyers almost always involves some degree of experimentation. If you are selling information, does it help to provide more sample information in the free area of the site that is available to everybody? For either goods or services, is it useful to offer "loss leader" products, getting the purchase process started with a very attractive offer and then betting that the buyer will include other, higher-margin goods in the purchase? Do special, limited-time offers induce more people to buy and then keep them coming back? Does providing more information about the product help sell it? There is no one answer to any of these questions for all companies. The right answer for you depends on how unique the product or service is, where you are drawing visitors from, how you differentiate your offer from competing offers, and many other factors. But, in all cases, being able to answer the question of how you turn lookers into buyers is critical to shaping your web business.

For virtually all companies closing sales on the web, making the purchase process quick and easy is also a critical part of success. National Semiconductor, for example, has been able to bring the average number of pages viewed between entry onto the site and a transaction down from over 7 to just over 2. We will look at just how National did this in a later chapter; the short answer is that the company personalizes the site for each customer, using profile information and past-purchase history, so that, when the customer returns to the site, the new components that are most probably of interest are displayed on the first page. In talking with engineers who shop for parts on the Internet, we consistently hear that the ability to find what they need very quickly causes many of them to go to National for sample parts. Log files, coupled with cookies or some other way to reconstruct visits, allow you to keep track of just how much trouble it is to complete a transaction on your own site. It is important to see the selection and purchase process through the buyer's eyes. Ideally, like National Semiconductor, you want to be able to put the product that the customer needs up on the first page that he or she sees.

All of these selling issues tie into the matter of returning customers. Clearly, making the buying process fast and efficient is easier if you already know something about the buyers, even if it is only their shipping addresses. Better yet, you can anticipate their tastes and needs.

Despite the obvious importance of cultivating and serving the return customer, we know of substantial web business sites that don't even bother to recognize returning customers. We know of many others that have given only scant consideration to whether returning customers differ from one-time or very infrequent buyers and to how they might go about developing more returning customers. Log files are a part of what you need to start answering such questions since they show you how the customer interacts with your site.

Selling Access to Visitors

A business that is just trying to close sales on the web wants to make it possible for the visitor to get on the site, do the deal, and get off the site as quickly as possible. On the other hand, a business that is focused on selling access and advertising wants customers to come onto the site as soon as they fire up their web browsers and then stay there all day. Not surprisingly, these differences in focus translate into different questions asked by the people trying to run the web business.

Let's look a little more closely at the issues and concerns confronting a business that wishes to make money by selling advertising and lead generation on the web. Revenues increase if you can

- Have a lot of visitors on the site at any given time.
- Know enough about the visitors so that you can give advertisers the ability to target specific audiences of interest and so that you can charge the higher rates associated with such targeted delivery.
- Get customers to click on the ad or in some other way identify themselves as a lead.

You get to know your visitors by having them spend a lot of time on your site looking at different content, initiating searches, clicking on ads to look at products, and then returning. You want to create a site that they use often, for news, industry information, purchasing, and entertainment.

There are different approaches to these goals. News organizations, including local newspapers, offer news, entertainment, community guides, and other services to attract an audience that will be of interest to local and regional advertisers. Search tools and portals, like Yahoo, provide visitors with guided access to the Internet, along with stock market quotes, weather forecasts, maps, and other information. All of this keeps visitors returning to the site, which, in turn, keeps advertising and sponsorship revenues flowing. Community sites, like Motley Fool, provide chat, specialized news, services, and feature articles targeted at the needs and interests of the community. Vertical portals focused on professionals in a particular industry, such as pulpandpaperonline.com or adhesivesandsealants.com, provide industry news, information about new products, information about job openings, and so on. Running across all of these different approaches is a common theme: Attract a large number of visitors, understand their interests, and keep serving them so that they keep returning.

These needs can be expressed in a small number of issues and related questions that companies engaged in this kind of business should be able to answer:

- **Value.** What is it that visitors value about the site?
- **Usage patterns.** Does use change over the course of the day or week? Does it change in response to outside events?
- **Intensity of use.** How much time do users spend in different areas of the site? Are there pages that get read fully? Are there ones that cannot hold the visitor's attention?
- **Where and why they leave.** There are good ways for visitors to leave, such as clicking on an advertisement or following a link out to a sponsor's site. There are also bad exits, such as when visitors just drift away. Are there patterns to departures that we can use to do a better job of keeping visitors on the site or sending them to an advertiser or a sponsor?
- **Demographics.** What can we know about the visitors that allows us to serve them with even more useful content and that increases their value to advertisers and sponsors?

The first three questions, regarding what it is about the site that visitors value, usage patterns, and usage intensity, grow out of the basic questions that apply to all businesses. But since we know our goal is to engage visitors and keep them on the site rather than enabling them to complete a sale efficiently and move on, we can approach the questions with a more focused perspective than we could when we were just looking at the general case.

One community site that we know of, focused on personal investing, knows that it is the discussion groups that are the heart of its business simply because that is where all the site activity is. One news site, on the other hand, finds that the really heavy traffic varies over time in response to news events. It has discovered that it can extend the peaks of traffic surrounding an external event by focusing on background information and related, "tie-in" stories coupled to big news events. The tie-ins provide attractive, predictably strong advertising opportunities. These kinds of insights should be readily available from your log files. The only requirement is being able to ask the right questions.

Questions regarding intensity and style of use are also answerable through straightforward log file analysis. Most commercially available programs include logic that can estimate the amount of time, on the average, that visitors spend looking at a particular page. The method is only an approximation, of course, since, as you now know, it is difficult to keep track of an individual's identity throughout a visit. But even the approximations show you which pages get a careful reading and which warrant only a quick, cursory look.

Many sites strengthen their ability to know when articles are really getting read by breaking articles into distinct pages that are linked together. The reader has to click a "Next page" button to move from one page to another. If there are nearly as many visitors looking at the last page as at the first, you can be pretty sure that most of the visitors are reading the article or, at the very least, printing a copy of it.

Through the use of the referrer information in the log file, it is possible to construct a picture of the paths that users take through your site. As noted earlier, the approach is at least superficially analogous to studying the direction and frequency of foot traffic by looking at the paths worn in a grassy field. One of the interesting questions is "Where do the paths end?" Unlike foot traffic, website visitors can suddenly disappear into thin air. It is sometimes useful to look at the pages from which they most often disappear. If the page is a logical terminal destination, such as a weather forecast, it is sometimes useful to ask what else you might put on that page to keep the visitor engaged (e.g., today's headlines from the city for which the forecast is requested). If it is not an obvious terminal page, it might be worthwhile to ask whether there is a potential mismatch between the visitor's expectations and the actual experience with that page that would cause the visitor to leave the site at that point. For example, does the page contain a lot of graphics and take a long time to appear on the screen for users coming in over a phone line and modem? Might they have gone to the page expecting to find some particular information (e.g., in-depth information about a company) and then received something else or something less (e.g., the page just has a quick, generic summary about the company)?

Knowing more about your visitors can potentially make your site more attractive for advertisers. Some of the information about visitors can come directly from their behavior on the site, as captured in the log files and as implied by the content that you offer. For example, if they are using a mortgage rate calculator on your site, it is a good bet that they are thinking about mortgages. You should be able to get premium rates from mortgage banks and brokers wishing to advertise on that page.

Log files also can tell you something about your visitors by showing you where they are coming from. If a good percentage of your traffic is coming to your site from links on the *Wall Street Journal*, that information in itself tells you something important about your visitors.

Do you offer a search capability on the site? Knowing which search terms are used most frequently is another insight into the interests and concerns of your visitors.

Moving beyond such relatively straightforward profiling information requires reaching beyond simple log file data. You can learn more about your visitors by offering them ways to personalize the site, thus making it more useful to them. Are there certain kinds of news and information that they want to see immediately, as they first enter the site? Are there updates, announcements, or news summaries that they would like to receive in e-mail? Answers to these kinds of questions can tell you even more about your visitors. We will look at just how to do this in great detail later in this book.

Registering for e-mail updates is interesting in ways that go beyond the simple list of subjects in which the visitors are interested. Knowing someone's e-mail address gives you a much more complete clue to his or her identity than is available through a simple IP address in a log file. What other information might be provided voluntarily during the registration process? (Remember, if he or she gets some advantage or benefit in return for providing you with the information, you are much more likely to actually get it.) Once visitors are registered, you can very probably place a cookie on their computers so that you can recognize them as they return to your site, providing you with yet more opportunity to build a useful visitor profile as you keep track of their activities from visit to visit.

Finally, there are specialized services that can work with you to develop demographic profiles of your visitors. These services go well beyond simple log file analysis, tying together information about visits to your site with other sites to produce much broader, richer profiles of the people coming to your site. The services are able to provide this information because they have built up a database of information about the different sites visited from a particular computer and therefore, typically, by one person or a small group of users. We will look more closely at how such services are able to go about collecting such information in Chapter 6. The important thing to note in the context of our discussion about key questions for your web business is that such broad demographic information is available through third parties.

Supporting a Non-Web Business

Most businesses, particularly existing businesses, are not primarily focused on using the web to close sales or to create revenue opportunities by providing other companies with access to buyers. Instead, their web business exists to support the primary, non-web business. Not surprisingly, this changes the questions that are used to understand how the business is connecting with customers on the web.

There are many ways to use the web to support a primary non-web business. The number and the variety of approaches have expanded greatly over the past few years as companies have become more sophisticated in their use of the web. Currently, the support mechanisms typically fall into one or more of the following four categories:

1. **Promotion.** This is where most companies start in their use of the Internet. The website serves as yet another kind of marketing collateral, telling potential customers about the company and its products.
2. **Lead generation.** This is the next step beyond promotion. Once you have visitors interested in the product and looking at your site, you convert them into leads that you can turn over to your sales organization.
3. **Support for the sales and distribution channel.** Whether you are selling directly through your own sales team or indirectly through distributors and resellers, the sales channel needs information and logistics support. The Internet is a good vehicle for providing at least some of this support.
4. **Customer relationship management (CRM).** Once you have made a sale, you need to support your customers with access to information about their

accounts, service information, technical support, news about the product line, product updates (e.g., new control software), and access to the community of other customers. The Internet can potentially improve such services while bringing down their cost.

Most companies start with the simplest functions, promotion and lead generation, and add channel support and CRM as they gain experience and make more investment in the web dimension of their business. Consequently, companies active at the more sophisticated end of this spectrum are also still using the website for promotion and lead generation. Let's look at an example of one company that is actively using all four of these approaches. The example will help us do a better job of framing the key questions and issues associated with tying web operations into your primary non-web business.

Nortel Networks is a networking hardware manufacturer that sells much of its product through distributors and value-added resellers. The company's primary competition sells directly to the end customer over the web; consequently, the use of a third-party channel is potentially an important way for Nortel to provide services and support that are not readily available from the competitor. One key question for Nortel is how the Internet can be used to support an indirect channel without undermining it.

In working with an indirect channel, there are, in general, two different kinds of communication that one can conduct over a website. The first is information that is sent directly to the third-party resellers and distributors and hidden from end-point customers. Such information is designed to help the resellers and distributors do a more effective job of selling. Examples include pricing and product information, marketing materials, sales training information, and other sales and service support information.

This first kind of communication is "safe" from the standpoint of protecting the role of the distribution channel, but it leaves too many competitive opportunities unexplored. Buyers expect to be able to go to the website of a company, particularly a high-tech company, and find at least basic information about the product directly, without having to work through a distributor. This leads to the second kind of communication available to Nortel and any other company that sells indirectly, which is communication directly to the end customer.

It is important to recognize that companies like Nortel can really benefit from such direct contact with customers. One of the frustrating things about selling through an indirect channel is that it is difficult to get firsthand information about how customers are using your products, what they like, and what they would like to see changed. Direct contact with potential customers over the Internet offers an opportunity to obtain such information. Unfortunately, it also provides an opportunity to inadvertently undermine your distribution channel.

Nortel decided to address this opportunity and the attendant risks by conceiving of its website as a way to build a more complete picture of its business, very much in the sense that we have been talking about in our discussion so far. What is it that buyers want to know about the Nortel products? Where do they need help? How can their use of the site tell Nortel more about their use of the product? What are they interested in buying?

This focus on getting a better understanding of its business means that Nortel is managing two objectives on its website as it engages the end customer. The first, of course, is to provide prospects and customers with the information that they need. The second is more complex: In the course of providing this information to end customers, Nortel gathers information that is useful in designing the products and in understanding customer needs and concerns.

In the course of interacting with end customers, Nortel also collects information that is useful for its partners and distributors. Such information includes everything from sales leads to insights into emerging customer interests to concrete facts about product applications. In short, rather than depending on the traditional information flow leading from the customer through the distributor to the manufacturer, Nortel is now using its website to run the loop in the other direction, from customer through manufacturer and then back to the distributor.

It is useful to take a closer, more concrete look at some of the things that Nortel has done to gather information from its website. Two initiatives stand out. The first is a comprehensive effort to provide technical support on the website. Building on top of a sophisticated document management system, Nortel provides end-user customers not only with online manuals but also with current reports of all known problems encountered by other customers, along with suggested solutions or work-arounds. Putting this information up on the website is good both for the customer and for Nortel. By monitoring page usage data, Nortel is able to gauge the frequency and, to some extent, the severity of the problems currently encountered in the field. This becomes an information resource that Nortel can turn back around to the distribution channel so that it can proactively offer customers better service.

The second interesting initiative is a product *configurator.* Networking hardware is not just a simple, sealed-up box. It typically consists of a set of interrelated components that are assembled to build the final installation used at the customer's site. A typical installation might include a power supply, a supervisory and control module, interface modules, and router and switch modules, all assembled into an appropriate chassis. Making sure that an order includes all of the components needed for a particular application and that the components will work with one another is an important part of ensuring customer satisfaction.

Before the Internet, product configuration was one of the services supplied by the distributors and resellers. It was a necessary service as well as an expensive one, as the distributors had to stay up to date on all of the configuration possibilities and constraints for a complex product line. So Nortel built an online system that automatically walks a buyer or prospect through the configuration process, working step by step through the constraints and choices. In addition to ensuring that the configuration gets done right, the online configuration process helps the buyer see and appreciate the flexibility of the overall system and the range of functions that it can support.

Once the prospect has created a particular configuration, he or she can save it and print it. This becomes a tool for the buyer that can be used to speed up the ordering process from the distributor or reseller. It is also a lead generation tool since Nortel can send the completed order to a distributor, along with contact information optionally supplied by the buyer. And, finally, it is a way for Nortel to get much better insight into what customers are actually doing with the product. In the old, pre-Internet days, when the company sold through distributors and depended completely on information coming back through those distributors, Nortel might know only that it was delivering so many dozen chassis and so many hundred modules of different kinds to a distributor. It did not know, except anecdotally, how all of those pieces were going together on the customer's site. Now, in the course of helping with configuration online, Nortel knows in detail which components are being used together—information that can help the company make better product design and pricing decisions, all while supplying better information to distributors.

It is also interesting to note that Nortel, in providing basic product and configuration information over the Internet, discovered that the effect of these new services on distributors and resellers was far from uniform. The distributors who were themselves providing little value beyond information about products and configuration found that they needed to redesign their offerings. Nortel provides the training and guidance to help these weaker distributors. Other distributors, however, found that the new Internet services have helped their businesses grow.

Freed from the costs of providing relatively low-value services, they have been able to focus on higher-value, higher-paying services such as those tied to specific applications of the company's hardware.

One lesson from this small case study is that you should try to find ways to make information flow both ways. When you are using the web to address critical functions requiring delivery of information to customers, that should also be a way for you to learn more about those same customers. It is the two-way communication that begins to build real customer engagement.

A second lesson is that the critical ways in which the web can support your primary business—promotion, lead generation, channel support, and customer relationship management—can be usefully connected so that each function supports the others. What ties the functions together is the flow of information. Watching customer response to promotions generates sales leads that can be passed to the channel. Data collected during product configuration is another source of sales leads but also assists in customer support. Providing a rich support environment for the end customers keeps them coming back to the site, creating more opportunities for promotion and lead generation. What ties all of these functions together are the answers to the basic questions we have been looking at throughout this chapter: How many people are coming to the site, who are they, what are they doing, and what do they seem to want?

Mixes and Blends of Web Business Models

We have looked at three different approaches to web business: closing sales on the website, selling access to web visitors to other companies, and using the web to support sales and growth of your non-web business. Although there are nice logical distinctions among these business models, most companies, in practice, approach the web through a mix of the models. They sell some product directly on the web, they use the web to support their traditional non-web business, and they may also sell some advertising or generate leads for partners. Such mixed models can work just fine, but they can also be a significant source of difficulty and confusion.

The difficulty arises when managers think of such a mixed-model web business as if it were one thing, with one set of objectives. There are, of course, many senses in which the web business really is one thing, particularly when viewed within the overall revenue operations of a larger company. But, if the business mixes basic web business models, perhaps combining selling with community building and lead generation, it is very important to remember that measuring and analyzing the operation's success requires consideration of a variety of metrics and objectives. It does not, for example, make sense to ask whether visitors are spending enough time on the site unless you specify which part of the site, with which objectives, you are talking about. If you are looking at the direct selling part of the site, the faster the customer completes the sale and gets off the site, the better. If you are looking at the community part of the site, the longer the customer stays, the better.

In working with a mixed-model web business, it is often useful to ask whether you have the mix of proportions right as you combine the models. One web business that we know of started off selling magazine subscriptions on its site and also sold advertising for other products because the selection of a magazine was a useful indication of buyer interest and preferences. For example, someone looking at *Mustang and Fords* magazine is probably a good, well-qualified prospect for advertisers offering rebuilt vintage Mustang parts. This business learned that the different dimensions of its business model, though apparently complementary when viewed at a high level, did not necessarily fit together in terms of focusing the site on a particular customer behavior. From the magazine subscription perspective, the goal was to get the visitor to put the *Mustang and Fords* subscription in the shopping cart and then to show the visitor other magazines that might be of interest to try to increase the value of the sale. From the advertising perspective, the goal was to get the user to click on the ad, leaving the magazine site and perhaps abandoning the shopping cart. The company eventually decided to stop accepting advertising. In this case, the right proportions for mixing the business models eventually turned out to be all or nothing. In other cases, the mixes might be more complex, using different parts of the site for different kinds of activity. The important thing is to realize that you *are* mixing models, and getting things right means finding the right mix.

An interesting class of web business model hybrid that is emerging rapidly enough to deserve special treatment is the business that creates net markets. The key to these businesses is that they address product information and distribution problems in fragmented markets, where buyers have a hard time comparing information from different sellers. For instance, one such company is using the web to provide buyers with access to a database of repair parts for ships that is organized by the form and function of the parts. Whenever possible, the company will offer to complete the sale of the part on the website and to then arrange credit terms, insurance, and shipping for the part. This is an attractive idea because it is currently sometimes difficult for shipowners to locate a particular repair part or replacement system, particularly for older ships. Creating a worldwide supply network, coupled with powerful searching, addresses a real problem for the buyers.

How does such a web business make money and grow? Part of the answer has to do with closing sales, making it as easy and as fast as possible for a port engineer to locate the right part, purchase it, and arrange for its delivery. In such an instance, revenue comes from taking a commission from the sale. Building traffic on the site may require more than just a parts exchange, however. It may be useful to offer news about the shipping industry, coverage of new technical developments in the ship repair business, and perhaps even postings of employment opportunities for port engineers and others involved in the ship maintenance and repair business. Using the current buzz phrase, it might make sense for this company to grow into a vertical portal focused on ship repairs, building the portal around the core business of providing a parts exchange.

Following such a hybrid course means creating an intentional mix of web business models. The core business focuses on closing sales on the web. The supporting dimensions of the business focus more on creating a community of regular visitors. Revenues from that community could come from advertising and lead generation for parts suppliers and repair service providers. As in the magazine site, advertising and lead generation do not necessarily fit together well with the "closing sales" function. On the other hand, they support the community function, which may, in turn, support the sales function.

As in other specific instances of web businesses that we have looked at, there is not a black-and-white, right-or-wrong answer to the question of how best to blend the different web business models to create an effective, profitable portal for marine repair supplies and services. What there is, instead, is a need to be able to break apart the different dimensions of the web business, to articulate the purpose of each part, to measure results in terms of those purposes, and then to look at how the business dimensions interact, sometimes supporting one another and sometimes getting in one another's way. Focusing on the different business models, tied to different revenue streams, gives you a way to do that.

Summary

There are only a small number of basic models for making money on the web; you should decide which model best fits your business. For each model, there is a set of fundamental issues and questions that should direct your data collection and analysis: The point of the analysis is to answer the key questions for your kind of web business.

If your business depends on closing sales on your website, you are primarily interested in understanding what differentiates lookers from buyers and in how to turn lookers into buyers. You also want to figure out how to make the buying process as fast and as simple as possible. Making buying easy is partly a matter of looking at the steps that buyers must take and then streamlining that process. It can also build off of knowing more about what your buyers want. Pursuit of some of these questions requires keeping track of visitor identity, at least anonymously, and so requires the use of cookies or some other way to identify a user throughout a session on the site. It can also be helpful to tie the log file information into a registration database.

Businesses that depend on advertising or other revenue from generating leads or linking visitors to other sites have a set of concerns that are, in some ways, just the opposite of the issues facing sites that sell directly on the web. Here, the focus is on getting people to the site and keeping them there for as long as possible. While they are on the site, you want to learn as much as you can about them. The data in log files can be a big help in understanding what people value about your website by looking at where they spend their time and at how much time they spend with particular pages. It is equally interesting to know how people move through the site and whether there are departure points away from the site that could be changed in some way to lead people back into the site. Log file data, once again, can help with such questions. However, you are probably also interested in knowing when customers return to the site. This question requires use of cookies or a registration database to answer. Cookie information, coupled with third-party services, can also be used to develop demographic profile information for the site.

The most common form of web business is one that supports another non-web business operation. Support functions typically include promotional activities, lead generation, sales and channel support, and customer relationship management. Companies that have developed capabilities in each of these areas find that they support one another and that the connective tissue between the operations is built up from customer information. Website activity data is one of the key inputs into the store of customer information.

Many businesses mix together the different web business models, selling some product directly, supporting a non-web business, and perhaps building a community of users. In pursuing such a course, it is critically important to be able to clearly identify which parts of the web business are working with which models and to be able to clearly state the intended way in which the different business models will support one another. In short, it becomes necessary to articulate the more complex expectations associated with the more complex business. The importance of checking to see whether these expectations are being met is heightened by the likelihood that the different business models will, in fact, conflict with one another unless they are carefully designed and managed.

Key Ideas

- There are actually a small number of basic ways to make money on the web. They include selling goods and services directly, selling access and leads for others with goods and services, and using the site to support operations that produce revenue off the web. The goals and operations of the models differ in important ways, leading to different kinds of website data collection.
- When you are using the web to support your non-web business, which is perhaps the most common form of web business, it is the interactions with the end customer that often tie together the different goals and functions of the website. Customer information, gathered through log file data and through closer kinds of customer engagement, becomes the central resource that you manage.
- Most companies mix business models to some degree. Be aware that the goals and requirements of the different models can easily conflict with one another. Consequently, it is important to be able to state why you are mixing models and what each of the pieces of the business is supposed to do in relation to the others.

CHAPTER SIX

Using Cookies

Objectives of This Chapter

- Describe the important problem that cookies solve, explaining the original thinking behind creating them.
- Provide a clear idea of what is inside a cookie and of how cookies move between your company's web server and your customers' browsers.
- Show how cookies can help you support more complex interactions with your customers.
- Explain why there are security and privacy concerns surrounding the use of cookies.

We are at a pivotal point in our development of tools and approaches to customer engagement on the web. The chapters that preceded this one focused on looking at your customers in an aggregate sense. We have focused on the overall business model that you use as you move onto the web. Customer engagement has meant developing a good, general understanding of the needs of your customers and of how they see your business. Our metrics have consisted of frequency counts and trends. Our engagement has been an engagement with groups.

The chapters that follow will begin to shift the sense of customer engagement. We will move from looking at aggregations to considering the needs of individual customers. We will begin to develop serious approaches to "personalizing" the website and the customer's interaction with it.

This shift from the aggregate to the individual requires that we have a way to identify and recognize individuals. As we have already suggested in our earlier discussion of visits, cookies can be a critical part of the identification process. In this chapter and the next, we take a look at what cookies are and at some of the issues you will encounter as you use them.

There's Something about Cookies

There are users who really hate cookies. In an e-mail exchange, one user summed up his feelings on the matter by saying, "You might as well just tattoo a bar code across your forehead." Others are less firm in their opinions but are still uncomfortable about cookies: "Is there some way that hackers can use a cookie to get hold of my credit card number?"

On the other hand, we know that cookies are a potentially very useful tool. In particular, they give us a way to pull together the page views that make up visits. Within limits, they can even help signal when a particular computer is being used for return visits.

So, just listening to the assertions and counterassertions, it would appear that cookies are perhaps a serious threat to privacy and, at the same time, a very important tool for any web business.

Sorting out the claims and counterclaims is much easier if we can start with a straightforward, factual description of what a cookie is and of how web servers and browsers use cookies. Working from that foundation, we can look at how businesses can use cookies to keep track of information in ways that should not concern any user. We can also examine ways to use cookies that do, in fact, aggregate information that might be viewed by some users as an invasion of privacy.

We will begin our discussion of cookies by looking at the communications between web servers and web browsers, at where cookies fit into these communications, and then at the structural makeup of cookies. These explanations are not intended for an audience of engineers. Business managers, too, need a general understanding of why cookies were invented and at how they are made in order to make good decisions about putting them to use.

Stateless

One of the brilliant things about the HTTP protocol, which underlies communications on the World Wide Web, is that it is *stateless,* meaning that a web server can treat each and every request for a page or a graphic as an independent event. The reason that this matters is that keeping track of context—knowing where you are in a chain of connected events—is expensive and difficult when you are trying to handle thousands of transactions at one time. The stateless architecture of the web is one of the reasons why it scales well.

Not surprisingly, there are also disadvantages associated with making things quick and simple. The *good* thing about being able to keep track of state is that it allows you to break transactions into pieces. Think about what you have to do when you get cash from a bank machine:

1. Identify yourself and your account by inserting a card.
2. Choose a language for the interaction.
3. Provide your pass code.
4. Say whether you want to withdraw funds or make a deposit.
5. Indicate the account from which you want to withdraw.
6. Say how much you want to withdraw.
7. Choose whether or not you want a receipt.

Imagine having to do all of this on a single screen. It would make for a very confusing interaction, with too many choices all at once. By breaking the transaction into a number of screens, the automated teller machine is able to use your choices on previous screens to narrow down the options you need to see on subsequent screens.

The reason that it is possible for the ATM to work across multiple, sequential screens is that it can keep track of the state of your transaction as you proceed. For example, as it presents a series of screens to handle steps 4 through 6 in the sequence just given,

- it knows that you are the same person from step to step (because there is only one user interface on the ATM and it still has your card).
- it remembers your answer from the previous step as it presents the next step.

Although neither of these achievements is rocket science—they are the kinds of things that you just expect a computer to be able to do—both are beyond the ability of the basic HTTP web protocol. Since the web is stateless, each interaction between the server and your browser is a whole new world as far as the web server is concerned. We saw the result of this statelessness in our study of the records in log files. Each record is a separate event. The best we can do when we are just looking at IP addresses and page views is to say that a sequence of records is *probably* connected. As the word *probably* implies, the connections from record to record, screen to screen, are certainly not reliable enough to allow us to support withdrawal of funds from someone's checking account.

Getting cash from a bank machine is actually a very simple transaction. If the web's stateless protocol gets in the way of such simple commerce, how can we do much more complicated things, such as support online applications for mortgages? The answer is that we need to supplement the basic HTTP protocol by adding a way to keep track of the state of an interaction. Cookies were added to the browser/server interaction to address just that problem.

Cookie Communications

Before we dive into the matter of how cookies are set, it is helpful to have a general idea of just what a cookie is: It is a small amount of data sent from a web server to a web browser. The browser saves this small data package by writing it to the disk on the browser's host machine. The next time that the browser makes a request from that same website, it sends the data (the cookie) back to the server. In a sense, the server is saying, "I am stateless and can't remember things, and so I won't know where we are in our conversation when you return. So here is a reminder of where we left things. Keep it in a safe place and then send it back to me when you pick up the conversation again, and I will be able to carry on."

Understanding just how this interaction between the web server and the web browser happens is critical to understanding how cookies can be used. In particular, knowing who has permission to do what is critical to understanding the security and privacy risks associated with cookies. Figure 6–1 outlines the exchange of information between a browser and a web server as a cookie is set and returned.

One of the basic principles of web interactions is that web servers do not initiate communications with web browsers: The browser always starts the conversation. So things begin when the browser requests a web page from a website. If the website has been constructed to use cookies, the web server responds to the browser's request by sending the page accompanied by instructions to set a cookie. The browser can decide whether or not it wants to follow these instructions. We will look at the cookie management options on different browsers a little later; for now, it is sufficient to know that most browsers can be set up to ignore "Set Cookie" commands, to notify the user and ask for further instructions, or to set the cookie without comment.

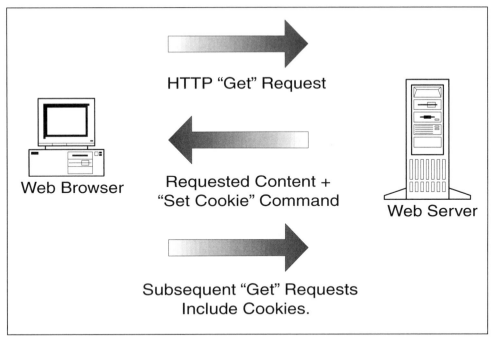

Figure 6–1 Setting and returning cookies

Now the cookie is recorded on the web browser's computer. How does it get back to the web server? Before a web browser makes any request from any website, it scans through its list of cookies to see whether any cookies are associated with the site being contacted. If there are, the browser sends all the cookies received from the site back to that same site. Working this way, the state information is sent

---

Technical Note: Sites and Servers

To keep the discussion and the language simple, we are not distinguishing between "website" and "web server" at the moment, acting as if a website had only a single server. In fact, of course, there can be many servers supporting a website. From the browser's standpoint, if you have seen one server on a site, you have seen them all. We will look more carefully at ways to restrict the return of cookies later in this chapter, but, for now, we are assuming that if a cookie came from a particular site, the browser will send it back with all requests directed to that site.

from the server to the browser, saved by the browser, and then returned to the server with each subsequent request. The cookie is passed back and forth as the conversation continues.

A Cookie Example

All of this talk about states and communication is pretty abstract, but it has very practical applications. Consider the fact that if you go onto almost any retail shopping site, you can select things and put them into a "shopping cart," collecting a number of purchases before you check out. On most sites, you can do this without registering or identifying yourself. How does this work? If the site is a busy one, your requests for pages are reaching the server at nearly the same time as hundreds, perhaps thousands, of other requests. If you are coming in from someplace like AOL, your IP address may be the same as that of many other people who are shopping at the same time. We know that, from a log file perspective, sorting out your actions from those of the hundreds of other shoppers is essentially impossible. Yet your cart ends up only with your selections, rather than those of other shoppers with the same IP address. How does this happen?

The answer is that your "cart" is really a cookie, or sometimes a set of cookies, stored on your own computer. The cookies collect the information about the successive "states" of your shopping trip as you proceed. Figure 6–2 shows how this might work for someone buying a backpack and sleeping bag on an outdoors equipment site.

This example illustrates a couple of important points about cookies. The first, of course, is that they do actually succeed in tying together the different steps of the visitor's interaction with the website. They provide the "memory" that turns the web's stateless interactions into a real visit—something that has a duration and that changes over time.

The second important thing to note is that the web browser returns all of the cookies associated with the site with *every* "Get" request. You may remember from our discussion of log files that the display of a single web page might require a dozen or more separate "Get" requests, one for every image, including bullets and other small graphics. There are also separate requests for every style sheet reference and for every other file used in the construction of the page. Whether the browser is asking the server for key content or just for the image file for a bullet, it sends off *all* the cookies associated with the site with *each* request. Clearly, if you have a lot of cookies or if the cookies are large files, all of this mostly pointless communication can slow things down.

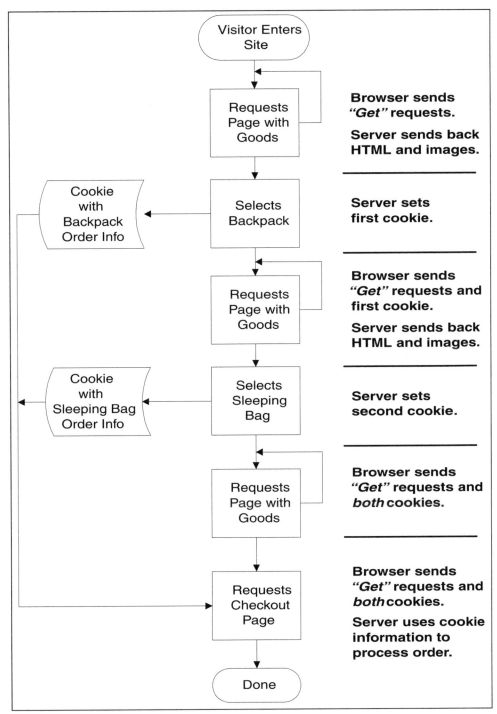

Figure 6–2 Use of cookies to implement a shopping cart

Technical Note: Implementation Details

This example, along with this discussion in general, is intended to provide you with a sense of what cookies do and why they are important. If you were implementing a system, there are a number of design choices that you could make that might be important in your implementation. We note them here just for completeness. They do not change the substance of our example.

The first detail is that you might choose to collect shopping cart entries in a single cookie. Rather than setting a new cookie for each transaction, you could simply add the new purchase information to the end of the cookie by rewriting it. Choosing between the approaches is a design decision that would vary from application to application. We used the multiple-cookie approach in our example to illustrate the fact that the web browser can end up sending back more than one cookie with each request.

A second point is that there is no constraint that requires all the different cookies for a site to be the same. You will often use a cookie to hold relatively permanent information, such as a customer ID number, and then use other cookies for more transient purposes, such as collecting the contents of a shopping cart. The browser sends all of the cookies back to the server with each request, no matter what their structure and purpose.

Finally, and perhaps most usefully, you can set cookies from scripts within the browser client, as well as from within the server. In other words, the "Set Cookie" command does not always require communication between the browser and the server. Instead, a script running within the web page can operate locally, running just on the client, and set the cookie. This has the advantage of cutting down on communication time and can make use of the client's computing power, thus decreasing the load on the server. This approach is useful for scripted applications, including some shopping cart applications, where the visitor can make a number of decisions on the page. Note that whether cookies are set by the client as it runs a script or are set directly by the server, they are all returned to the server with the next "Get" request from the client.

In sum, cookies are a way to tie together the separate page requests from a browser to a website, keeping track of the changing state of the transaction. They are stored on the client machine but can be set by the server. The client returns them to the appropriate server with each and every request.

Our next step is to understand what is inside a cookie and to find out about security—that is, who can do what with a cookie? That means looking at the data fields contained in a cookie.

What Is in a Cookie?

The recipe for cookies is simple and contains only a few ingredients. They are designed to be small objects that can be sent back and forth quickly. Table 6–1 lists the fields in a cookie and provides a brief description of each field.

Table 6–1 Cookie Structure

Field	Description
Domain	Identifies the site that stored the cookie. For example, a cookie set from the Addison Wesley Longman site might contain ".awl.com". When the browser makes requests of the site identified in this domain, it will return the cookie with the request.
Path	Allows the designer to tell the browser to send cookies back to only certain parts of the site. If you only need cookies along with requests in the membership part of your site and if all member material is under a subdirectory called "members," then you would set this field to "/members".
Secure	If set to a value, it allows cookies to be encrypted during transit to and from the server.
Expiration	Sets the time and date that the cookie will expire. On most browsers, a cookie without an expiration date lasts only until the user exits the browser program.
Name	An identifying name for the cookie.
Value	The information stored in the cookie—for instance, information about a purchase to create a shopping cart.

> ### Technical Note: Cookie Limits
>
> There are a number of limits associated with cookies. The limits are important because they underscore the purpose of cookies: They can't be very big, and you can't have thousands of them. The limits can differ between systems; the numbers here are what you can count on for most systems.
>
> | Parameter | Limit |
> | --- | --- |
> | Total number of cookies on a client | 300 |
> | Maximum size per cookie | 4K |
> | Maximum number of cookies returned to one domain | 20 |

Since we are not worried about writing programs to set cookies, we do not need to go into great detail about these fields and about how you set them. If such information is of interest, consult the references listed at the end of this chapter. Our focus, instead, is on the way that the contents of the cookie shape its use, particularly with regard to security and privacy. As someone running a business, you will want to know what security options are available to you. It is also important for you to see where problems could arise and how they can compromise privacy. Part of your task will be convincing users that your use of cookies does not threaten them in any way. Being convincing requires understanding the threat. We will begin by looking at a few of the most critical fields inside cookies and then will look at the actual contents of some cookies.

The "Secure" Field

Since we are interested in security, let's begin by looking at the "secure" field. The server that sets the cookie can specify that the cookie is to be sent back and forth using encrypted transmission, keeping others along the Internet route from reading the contents of the cookie. If this option is used, the secure field will have a value.

In practice, the secure option is rarely used; in looking at thousands of cookies received from different sites, I have yet to see a value in the secure field. The reason for this may be tied to a second feature of this security option, which is that it does not affect the way that cookies are stored on the client machine:

Today's browsers always store cookies in plain text, where they could be looked at by anyone with access to the machine, regardless of the setting of the secure field. Consequently, the only real security comes from encrypting the values of the cookie on the server by some other means. This may explain why nobody uses the secure transmission feature.

The important conclusion to draw from all of this is that it is completely reasonable for users to assume that any information placed in a cookie is generally available to prying eyes, unless the site that sets the cookie takes appropriate security precautions. This suggests that users should be cautious about taking cookies from strangers or, at least, from companies whose practices might not be rigorous and well thought out from a privacy standpoint. Being able to describe and explain your cookie practices to visitors is consequently an important part of gaining their trust.

The "Name" Field

The "name" field is simple but important. It identifies the cookie on the visitor's machine. Combined with the domain and path information, which says that the cookie comes from a particular server and applies to a particular area of the site, the name uniquely identifies the cookie. If you write a new cookie with the same name, domain, and path as an existing cookie, the new one overwrites the old one. This allows you to update cookie information.

The "Value" Field

Visitors are concerned not only about security but also about just what is kept in the cookie. The "value" field is the cookie's payload. Working within some limitations about the characters that you use (you cannot include spaces, semicolons, or commas, but you can use escape sequences as substitutes), the value can contain anything that you like, up to the maximum allowable size for cookies.

There are some commonsense guidelines that should guide decisions about what to put in value fields. In particular, you should not put anything in there that cannot be safely passed around on the Internet. However, not all companies sending cookies use common sense. This is an area where cookies, clumsily used, can become a privacy and security risk.

To make the case most dramatically, there is nothing that would prevent a site where you shop from deciding that it is convenient to store your name and credit card information in a cookie. Hey, then it is always available, right? Since cookies generally travel as clear text and are always stored as clear text, this would obviously be a very serious compromise of privacy. The good news is that we have never yet seen this happen. The bad news is that the end user is not driving the car here. The stupidity could all be on the side of the vendor, and the consequences primarily on the side of the user.

Stupidity, or carelessness, does happen. For example, we have seen name and password information for a site sent back and stored in a cookie in unencrypted plain text. Incredible? Sure, but the strangest part of this story is that this practice is conducted by a site run by one of the major industry trade magazines, and the purpose of the site is to provide news and information to information systems managers. Perhaps they are trying to teach the managers a lesson.

In general, the information stored in the value field is relatively short. It is often just an identifying key that the server can use to retrieve your records from a database, or perhaps it is some short, encrypted information. All of this will be less mysterious if we look at a few examples of cookies.

Some Sample Cookies

What appears in Figure 6–3 is a list of cookies created by a Netscape 4.0 browser. In each of these records, the first field is the *domain* to which the cookie will be returned. We will discuss the meaning and use of this field in a few moments.

The second is a special field (different browsers add their own fields to the standard set) that says whether the cookie was set from the server or from a script

```
.amazon.com      TRUE  /  FALSE  2082787017  ubid-main  6310-98948356
.wsj.com         TRUE  /  FALSE  1293839973  user_type  subscribed
.wsj.com         TRUE  /  FALSE  1293839876  WSJIE_LOGIN
        klsoiupoanuKeATAbDfBw11eufkerti
.nytimes.com     TRUE  /  FALSE  946684527   PW      1/,7=klkje
.nytimes.com     TRUE  /  FALSE  946684529   ID      <5228980f
.amazon.com      TRUE  /  FALSE  2082787185  x-main
        F4760rtC21zKY3F6Tmp1rM
.fastwater.com   TRUE  /  FALSE  945306745   fw-member  4632
www.eddiebauer.com FALSE  /  FALSE  1262321968  ShopperManager%2Feb
        SHOPPERMANAGER%2FEB=U06Qk1jhdfk2228A4H7TT0
.llbean.com      TRUE  /  FALSE  1025620596  LLBEAN  507830-
    email:7:931012609:9809890834:930108102
```

Figure 6–3 Part of a cookie file maintained by a Netscape browser

running on the client. In all cases but the Eddie Bauer cookie, the values of this field are *true,* indicating that they were set from the server. The Eddie Bauer cookie, which appears to be used to implement a shopping cart, was set on the client, as indicated by the *false* value.

The third field is the *path* field. This is another field that we will look at in a moment. For now, simply note that, in each case, the path is simply the "root," meaning that cookies will be returned with calls to any point on the domain site.

The fourth field is the *secure* flag. Note that none of these records uses secure transmission.

The fifth field records the *expiration* of the cookie. This is another important field that we will discuss in a moment. It is an enormous integer that represents expiration date in terms of the number of milliseconds after January 1, 1970, Greenwich mean time.

The sixth and seventh fields are the *name and* the *value* of the cookie, respectively. Let's look at a few of the examples to see how these sites are using the cookie values.

The Amazon cookie is a user ID. It is a way to look up a user's records in the Amazon database. As you can see by scanning down in the list, Amazon also uses cookies to keep track of other information about shopping and visiting activity.

The *Wall Street Journal* uses two cookies, one to tell its system that the person is a subscriber and the other to provide login information that is used to save users from the trouble of having to manually log in each time. Although you cannot tell this by looking at the list of cookies, it is worth noting that the *Wall Street Journal* gives users the option of setting the login cookie or not.

The *New York Times* is also using two cookies. One stores the subscriber's login; the other, the password. Both are encrypted. As with the *Wall Street Journal,* the *Times'* password cookie is offered to the user as an optional convenience.

The Fastwater cookie is another one that is simply an index key to support a database lookup.

We have already mentioned that the Eddie Bauer cookie appears to implement a shopping cart, very probably including item number, quantity, and size information.

The L.L. Bean cookie is interesting: It appears to encode user ID information with an encrypted e-mail address.

As you can see, most cookies are short and reasonably cryptic. Now, let's look at who and what has access to these cookies.

The "Domain" and "Path" Fields

Web browsers send cookies along with requests to particular web servers. A browser knows when to send cookies, and when not to, from the domain and path information stored in the cookies.

For example, let's look at the cookie set by Fastwater in the list of sample cookies in Figure 6–3. The "domain" field reads ".fastwater.com". Note the two periods, one before "fastwater" and the other preceding "com". One of the rules for domain fields is that the name must include at least two periods. That means that it is impossible to have cookies returned to any server with the suffix ".com", which would be a great many servers, indeed. The Fastwater cookie will be returned with requests to any domain ending with ".fastwater.com". This includes "www.fastwater.com", of course, but also "clients.fastwater.com", "trial.fastwater.com", and so on.

The Eddie Bauer cookie, on the other hand, will be sent back only with requests to "www.eddiebauer.com". If you were communicating with a server named, say, "service.eddiebauer.com", your browser would not send the Eddie Bauer cookies along with a request.

The number of requests that include cookies can be further restricted through use of the "path" field in the cookie. In the sample cookies of Figure 6–3, each of the cookies just uses "/" as the path. This means that cookies will be sent with any request to that domain since "/" represents the root node in the domain's directory structure. If you were setting cookies that were of interest only when a visitor was shopping, and if all shopping took place under a subdirectory on the site named "/store" (as in "www.sitename.com/store"), then you could set the path field to "/store" when creating the cookie. This would cut down on unnecessary cookie traffic when visitors were on other parts of the site.

The intent of the domain field is to make sure that cookies go only to the companies that set them. Amazon's cookies are returned only to Amazon, Eddie Bauer's cookies only to Eddie Bauer, and so on. It would be easy to defeat this intent if I could set a cookie with someone else's domain. I wouldn't be able to see someone else's cookies, but I could share mine. With a little coordination, it would then be easy to set up a central service that collects cookies from many places and that then compiles, analyzes, and redistributes this information about visitor behavior across sites.

To keep this from happening (as we will see in a moment, it *does* happen, but through another mechanism), browsers will only set a cookie with a domain address that matches the site that is issuing the "Set Cookie" command. The point is that, in most cases, cookies are simply a tool to conduct a conversation between one particular web business and one particular web browser. This is consistent with the purpose of maintaining the state of an interaction and should not cause anyone any serious privacy concerns, assuming that the content is encrypted or not generally meaningful (e.g., an index into a secure database).

The problem with this benign view of cookies is that there are, indeed, ways to use cookies to collect information across sites. We will examine them in a moment.

The "Expiration" Field

The "expiration" field holds the time after which the cookie should no longer be sent to web servers. Browsers differ in how they treat this field. Some will delete the cookie when it expires; others simply don't send it, but rather leave it on the disk. There are even browsers such as Lynx that take the aggressive view that cookies should not stick around at all and that therefore delete all cookies when the user exits the browser, regardless of expiration date.

It is possible to set a cookie without an expiration time. In this case, although browsers vary, the most common action is to treat the cookie as temporary, lasting only as long as that particular session (it is deleted when the user exits the browser). This is precisely what is needed for a cookie intended only to keep track of process state during a single transaction, such as when implementing a shopping cart. We recommend using such "one session only" cookies whenever it makes sense and then telling your visitors what you are doing and why.

Collecting Information across Sites

So far we have seen how cookies can be used to maintain the state of an interaction between a particular website and a particular client computer. Nothing that we have looked at, other than the fact that cookies are generally transmitted and stored as clear text, should raise any privacy concerns. So how is it that anyone could conclude that if you accept cookies on your browser, you might as well tattoo a bar code on your forehead?

The answer arises from the fact that what looks like a single web page can actually be a composite object built through the interaction of more than one Internet domain. Figure 6–4 shows how this works.

Suppose that the EdsBooks.com site contracts with KathysAds to sell advertising space on Ed's site. The EdsBooks page is, of course, served from the EdsBooks domain and so could only set cookies that would be returned to EdsBooks. But this page would contain a link to the KathysAds server so that KathysAds can send the GIF files or other information necessary to set up an ad. Because the visitor's browser is now communicating with the KathysAds server, KathysAds can also set a cookie—this time a cookie that will be returned to KathysAds.

Now suppose that FredsWine also contracts with KathysAds to sell advertising space. The FredsWine page also includes a reference to an ad that is delivered by the KathysAds server. Like EdsBooks, FredsWine can set cookies for its own use, and KathysAds can set cookies as it delivers the advertising.

The interesting thing, from KathysAds point of view, is that as the browser requests the ad for the FredsWine site, it returns the cookie set during the visit to EdsBooks. This cross-site cookie collection happens because browsers return cookies that belong to a particular domain, and, in each case, the advertising content comes from the same domain. This enables KathysAds to build an anonymous profile of the sites visited by a particular browser.

The mechanism that KathysAds would use to do this is simple. Suppose that the visitor goes to only these two sites, first to EdsBooks and then to FredsWine.

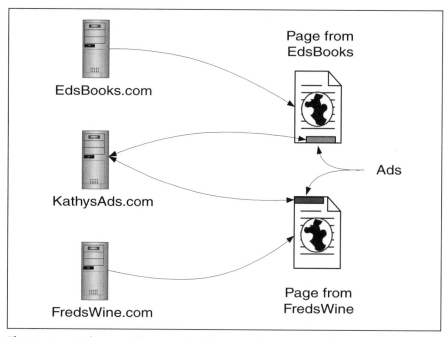

Figure 6–4 Using cookies to collect information across sites

On the visit to EdsBooks, KathysAds does not receive a cookie with the request for the ad but sets one containing three pieces of information in the value field: an identifying number for this browser, a number for the EdsBooks site, and an identifier for the particular ad that is displayed. Later, when the visitor goes to FredsWine, this cookie is returned to KathysAds along with the request for an ad. KathysAds can then note that this is a visitor who has been to EdsBooks. It also knows what ad was displayed there. By collecting and retrieving this information in a database, KathysAds can choose the next ad based on the record of previous ads and previous sites visited.

Over time, KathysAds builds up a resource that is of real value to its client companies. Let's assume that KathysAds also has contracts with sites focused on automobiles, news, political commentary, and so on. By building the user profiles in its database, the ad site can tell EdsBooks what percentage of its visitors is interested in wine, what percentage in automobiles, and what percentage in news and politics. Statistical analysis of the database will also allow KathysAds to see which sites group together, enabling construction of a market segmentation model for the visits from different client computers that are collected in the KathysAds database. It is important to note that cookies are tied to particular *computers* using a particular web browser rather than to the people who use them. If many people use a single computer and browser, the information collected by KathysAds for that computer/browser pair would not be a profile for any single individual. But since many computers are truly "personal" computers, much of the profile information could be of real value to the vendors using KathysAds.

The information collected by KathysAds gets quite interesting if it can be connected to the world of marketing information outside the Internet. KathysAds can do this by working out information exchange arrangements with its vendor clients. In particular, they need to agree to the use of the same identifying numbers for visitors so that when KathysAds references visitor 123456, the FredsWine records for that visitor use the same number. If this visitor registers with or buys something from FredsWine, the common number enables FredsWine to send the zip code to KathysAds. Including zip code information in the KathysAds database makes it much more valuable and useful since it can help establish the socioeconomic status of different groups of visitors.

But why stop at zip codes? If FredsWine has the user's name, phone number, and home address, why not exchange that information? It is just like swapping mailing lists, isn't it? Yes, except that, through the use of the common identifier, it is now possible to tie together information about Internet activity with other information about the magazines that the customer subscribes to, the clubs and organizations that he or she belongs to, and even the food he or she buys at grocery stores with a frequent buyer program.

Our examples so far have focused on business-to-consumer (B2C) applications, but the same approach can certainly be used in web companies selling in a business-to-business (B2B) environment. It doesn't even depend on advertising. Instead of KathysAds, we might start a company called "AnnsInfo" that does nothing but build the database of information about visitors and visits. AnnsInfo could serve a group of member companies, each of which agrees to make a call out to Ann's site to display a one-pixel image. This image is invisible to the user but does provide AnnsInfo with the opportunity to receive and set cookies and therefore to aggregate information across sites. Companies would subscribe to the AnnsInfo service because of the information that the service provides about the visitors coming to their sites.

Having done away with the dependence on advertising, AnnsInfo would be well positioned to serve business-to-business customers. Think back to the software company (CPS) that we looked at in Chapter 1. CPS was trying to sort out the value of the leads that it was generating from free software downloads. Profiling these visitors by knowing about the other sites that they were visiting would be very helpful in sorting out good prospects from less useful ones. For example, a visitor who was also spending time on the *Business Week* and *Wall Street Journal* sites and perhaps on the sites of other vendors selling web publishing systems software would probably be a more interesting prospect than someone who was visiting technically oriented tool sites.

Summary

Cookies are an essential addition to the stateless communication protocol that underlies the web. They enable you to construct interactions that grow and change over the course of a visit to your site. Examples of such interactions include shopping cart applications and the filling out of complex, multiple-page forms such as mortgage applications. Cookies also allow you to retain context between visits so that you can recognize returning visitors and customers.

The design of cookie interactions between a web browser and server includes features that provide for some degree of user privacy: In particular, cookies are sent back only to the server that set them. However, since it is the company setting the cookie that decides what to put in it, cookies do represent potential privacy and security risks if they are used carelessly by the company setting them. In addition, it is possible to construct web pages in such a way that cookies are returned to multiple servers during the display of a single page. The result is that it is possible to use cookies to collect information that ties together a person's activities across different websites, thus allowing companies to build profiles of user activity. Coupled with other identifying information, such as a zip code or even a name and address, that might be obtained from any one of the sites that someone visits, it is possible to use cookies as part of an effort to build fairly complete profiles of visitors.

How your customers regard such profile collection is an important question. We explore that issue in detail in Chapter 7.

Key Ideas

- Cookies are an important tool. If you want to sustain more complex interactions with website visitors—interactions that go beyond providing a series of disconnected page views—you will probably want to use cookies.
- Used carefully, cookies do not represent a privacy or security risk for visitors.
- Many users have concerns about cookies. Although some of the concern is probably based on not understanding what cookies contain and do, it is, in fact, possible to use cookies in ways that compromise privacy and security.
- One reasonable source of concern about cookies is tied to careless use of private, confidential information inside the cookie. Your website should include an explanation of just what you do with cookies.
- Another concern is tied to the potential for using cookies to collect information about activities across different websites. Given a little cooperation among vendors, usually centered on the need to serve ads, it is, in fact, possible to collect profiles of web browser activity across different sites.

Further Reading

If you are looking for more technical depth on the subject of cookies, I highly recommend Simon St. Laurent's *Cookies* (McGraw-Hill, 1998). It is an excellent complement to the material presented in this chapter. I have focused on meeting the needs of the business manager. St. Laurent focuses on the needs of the developer, providing detailed descriptions of how to set and use cookies using different languages and methods. The book contains scores of coding examples, as well as discussions of the idiosyncrasies encountered in working with particular tools in specific settings.

For a quicker, much shorter look at cookies from a technical perspective, the *Web Developer's Virtual Library* contains a number of short articles on cookies. For example, the article by Aaron Weiss titled "The State of State," which is located at **http://www.wdvl.com/Authoring/Languages/Perl/PerlfortheWeb/ state.html**, does a nice job of explaining why cookies are useful and includes some examples, written in Perl, of how to set and retrieve cookies.

Cookie Central, located at **http://www.cookiecentral.com/**, is an entire website dedicated to providing information about Internet cookies. It contains both general background information and news about new developments.

Another useful, though somewhat terse, technical reference is Netscape's specification for cookies, which is located at **http://home.netscape.com/newsref/ std/cookie_spec.html**.

Although there appears to be widespread general anxiety that cookies are being used to collect information about the activities of web users as they move from site to site, there are surprisingly few descriptions of how this actually works and of the role that ad servers play in aggregating the data (the sort of thing that KathysAds does in the example in this chapter). The general lack of understanding in this area is so large that one of the early reviewers of this book, while acknowledging that such cross-site collection was theoretically possible, offered his opinion that nobody would actually bother to do this. One article that does a good job of explaining what companies are currently doing in this area is Alan Zeichick's "Ad Serving Explained," which appeared in the January 2000 issue of *Red Herring*. In addition to telling you who is doing what, Zeichick offers some suggestions about how this area of web commerce will develop over the next year or two.

CHAPTER SEVEN

Privacy and Customer Engagement

Objectives of This Chapter

- Show why questions surrounding privacy and customer information, which include questions about the use of cookies, require management decisions, not just technical decisions.
- Make the connection between trust and the critical matter of your ability to engage the customer as an individual company or person.
- Provide a useful way of thinking about the connection between confidentiality of information on the one hand and benefit to the customer on the other.
- Assist you in developing a set of policies to guide your company's use of cookies.
- Suggest how you can use these policies to create greater comfort among your customers and business partners in your use of cookies.

Customer engagement builds on trust. If the customer does not trust your company, he or she will never provide you with the information you need to personalize the site to meet individual needs. Distrust will keep you from creating a close connection between the customer and your business.

In the preceding chapter, we noted that, for some customers, the very fact that you are using cookies creates distrust. We also saw that there are ways to use cookies, either through carelessness or through deliberate intent, that might reasonably cause concern about security and privacy among customers. In this chapter, we explore questions of trust and privacy in more detail. We show you what customers can do to frustrate your efforts to learn more about them. We also suggest an approach, based on mutual benefit, for you to build the kind of trust that will allow you to learn more about your customers so that you can serve them better.

Anticipating and Responding to Privacy Concerns

In Chapter 6, we looked at how three imaginary companies—EdsBooks, FredsWine, and KathysAds—could cooperate to build profiles of customer activity that looked beyond each company's individual website.

How one feels about this ability to build such complete profiles depends on which end of the relationship one is on. It also depends on one's feelings about privacy. If someone is trying to understand a web business, getting a better feel for who is visiting the site is very important. Consequently, the ability to collect information across sites sounds like a good deal. The kind of information collected by KathysAds in our imaginary example would obviously be useful to someone trying to make decisions about which other sites to advertise on or cross-link with. Since engaging a customer and providing personalized service require knowing that customer, it seems reasonable to try to learn as much as you can about the customer.

The website visitor, understandably, might not necessarily share the company's enthusiasm for knowing more about his or her needs and interests. Many businesses make the very critical mistake of forgetting that relationship and engagement involve two-way interaction. Remember, the fundamental maxim for web business is that the customer has new control and power. If customers do not like the fact that you are collecting information about them or do not like what you are doing with that information, they are gone.

There are two different dimensions to the customers' concerns about information that you collect. The first has to do with how personal and sensitive the information is. The second is tied to the benefit that customers receive from your having that information. Your success in collecting information to support customer engagement depends on working along both of these dimensions.

The dimension that reaches from anonymous information at one extreme to personal information at the other is a continuum. You should understand where your practices fall along this dimension. Most visitors have no objection to your uncovering truly aggregate, statistical information, such as the fact that a lot of the people visiting your site also visit some other site. Why would they care? But there is usually more of a sense of invaded privacy if, without a customer's permission, you make use of the fact that he or she is part of some group that you are tracking (e.g., "Here is yet another visitor who has also been to the EdsBooks site. Let's try to sell this visitor stuff that other people from EdsBooks have been buying."). So even if information is anonymous with regard to personal identity, using it without customer assent can cause problems. Finally, at the other end of the spectrum, is truly personal information that identifies the user. If you use such information in ways not anticipated by the user, without the user's permission (e.g., sell the user's name, address, and phone number to some other company that is building a central database), you are taking a substantial risk that visitors will feel that you have betrayed their trust.

The second dimension, which has to do with what the visitor gets out of the deal, is also a continuum. Customers are willing to trade away some privacy in order to get some tangible benefits. They provide phone numbers and other information to participate in frequent buyer programs at grocery stores because they get discounts on groceries. They participate in frequent flyer programs because they get credits that they can exchange for tickets or upgrades. You should expect visitors to ask, even if implicitly, what benefit they get from allowing your company to set cookies on their machines. If the cookies only last the length of a single session, the answer might be as simple as, "You get to use a shopping cart so that you can complete a purchase." If the cookie is persistent, lasting across sessions, the answer might simply be, "It saves you from having to reenter your password, shipping, and credit card information." On a business site the answer might be, "Your pricing is tied to your purchase volume, and this is how we keep track of what you have bought."

As the sensitivity and personal nature of the information that you want to collect increases, so must the benefit that the customer receives. If you want information about a corporate customer's purchasing requirements going forward, you had better be prepared to explain why giving you such information benefits that customer. The answer might be "By knowing more about your anticipated requirements, we can guarantee that what you need will be available when you need it." That answer needs to be explicit, however, and the customer needs to agree that the value received is commensurate with the information provided.

This exchange of benefit for information is at the heart of customer engagement on the web. We will look at just how web businesses build and use such transactions in subsequent chapters, as we look at different approaches to personalizing your site for customers.

Let's return, for the moment, to the matter of handling customer concerns about setting cookies on their computers. The key point is that cookies cannot be regarded as an issue that is separate from the larger engagement that you are building between you and your visitors. There is a range of things that you can do with cookies, and there is a range of benefits that your visitors can receive as a result. Creating engagement depends on getting the balance right so that the engagement is a win-win deal.

We can construct a graph from the two dimensions of the privacy equation that you control. (There are many other dimensions, such as policies set by the visitor's company and the visitor's own feelings about personal privacy, that you cannot control.) The result, shown in Figure 7–1, illustrates the range of alternatives open to you as you seek your visitors' cooperation in your use of cookies.

This diagram makes the point that a variety of choices are open to you. It also clearly illustrates the notion that as you increase or decrease your position on one scale, you should make appropriate adjustments on the other scale. Finally, and very

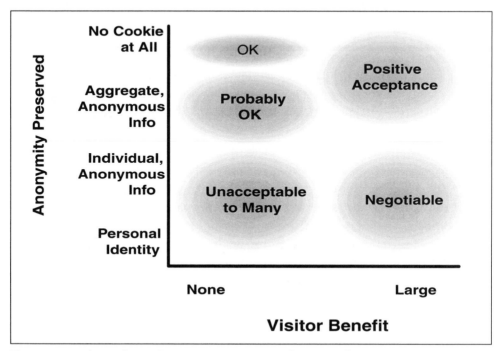

Figure 7–1 Dimensions of user response to cookies and privacy loss

critically, you can plan to target different positions on the graph with different customers over time. Your relationship with a customer is not static and does not have to always use the same mix of anonymity and benefit. As you work more with a customer, you are in a much better position to negotiate in a mutually beneficial way about the nature of your engagement. Much of the content of subsequent chapters is intended to help you think through the stages of that negotiation.

Cookie Defense

So far, we have been looking at cookies from the point of view of the web business that needs to use them. It is also useful to look at the visitor's options for managing cookies, inspecting them, accepting or rejecting them, and discarding them. Understanding the options and capabilities on the visitor's side is a basic requirement if you hope to have realistic expectations of what users will do with your cookies. It might even be in your interest to actively help customers select and use good cookie management tools since the better tools make it easy for customers to accept cookies from sites that they trust while still being more careful with less familiar sites.

Each web browser handles cookies a bit differently, and different versions of the browser from any single company can operate differently. All the same, it is useful to look at the general approaches taken in a couple of widely used products so that you can get a sense of how things look from the user's point of view.

Netscape Navigator 4

This is not the newest version of Netscape's browser, but it is the one that is in broadest use as of this writing. Adoption of new versions of browsers (you will remember that you can track such information in log files) has slowed down over the past few years. Consequently, it is a good bet that the version 4 browser will be the offer from Netscape that will be most commonly used for some time.

Netscape Navigator stores cookies in a single file. Figure 6–3, given previously, showed a fragment from such a file. It is a plain text file called "cookies.txt," which is usually found in a directory that Netscape Navigator sets aside for a particular user in the "Program Files\Netscape" directory. By looking at the file in Notepad or some other text-viewing tool, it is easy for any Netscape Navigator user to have a look at the cookies collected on his or her machine.

Netscape Navigator provides a number of options for controlling how the browser responds to requests to set cookies. These options are available from the "Preferences" window, as shown in Figure 7–2.

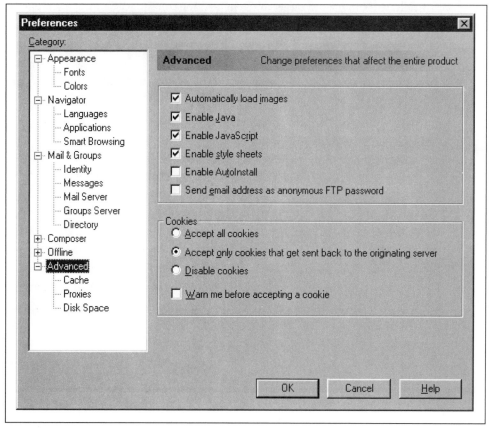

Figure 7–2 Netscape Navigator 4 options for controlling cookies

As you can see, the user can choose any of three options for accepting or rejecting cookies:

1. **Accept all cookies.** It does what it says: You get every cookie.
2. **Accept only cookies that get sent back to the originating server.** Netscape's description of this option implies that it addresses the problem of getting cookies that cross between sites, restricting the cookies to the site that provided the original page. This would be a great option if it worked. In practice, frames, scripts, and other devices still enable advertisers to set up the kind of "FredsWine, KathysAds" cross-site operation that was described in Chapter 6.
3. **Disable cookies.** All cookies are rejected.

The check box next to the option "Warn me before accepting a cookie" is important and useful. When this box is checked, you receive a message such as the one in Figure 7–3 before Netscape Navigator writes the cookie into the cookies file.

This message allows the user to see who is wanting to set the cookie and how long it will last. If it is just a cookie for the current session, there will not be date information. Because the warning identifies the server that is setting the cookie, a user can see whether this is a cross-site cookie.

The problem with the warning box from the user's point of view is that many sites are quite persistent about trying to set a cookie, even when you say no. The user can spend a lot of time clicking the "Cancel" button before actually getting to see the page. As we will see in a bit, there are third-party programs that can automate the process of saying "No, thank you."

Microsoft Internet Explorer 4

The dominant version of Microsoft's Internet Explorer is also version 4. It offers the cookie management options shown in Figure 7–4.

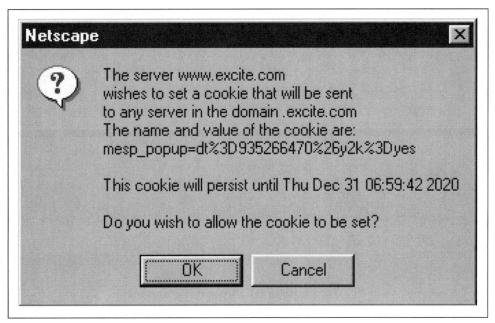

Figure 7–3 Netscape Navigator 4 cookie warning

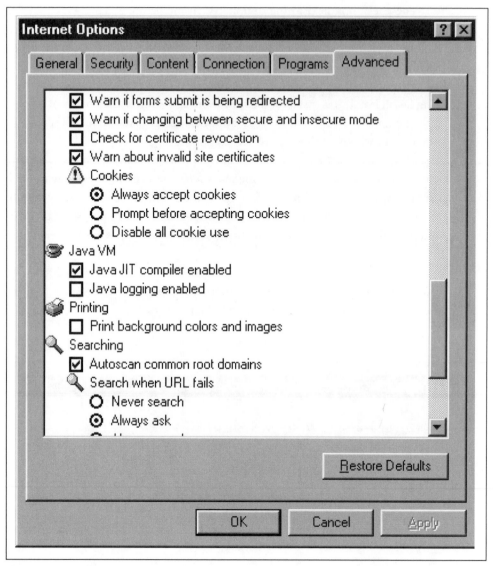

Figure 7–4 Microsoft Internet Explorer 4 cookie options (© 1999 Microsoft Corporation)

As you can see, this window combines the Netscape Navigator check box and accept/reject options into a single set of choices:

1. Always accept cookies.
2. Prompt before accepting cookies.
3. Disable all cookie use.

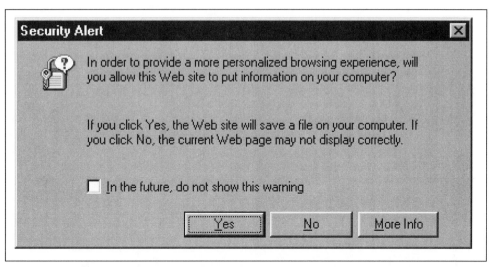

Figure 7–5 Microsoft Internet Explorer 4 cookie alert and prompt (© 1999 Microsoft Corporation)

If you choose the "Prompt before accepting cookies" option, Internet Explorer 4 puts up the prompt shown in Figure 7–5 when it receives a "Set Cookie" command.

Apart from the sales pitch about the "personalized browsing experience," there is not much here. However, when you click the "More Info" button, Internet Explorer 4 shows you a much more complete description of the cookie, such as the one shown in Figure 7–6.

As you can see, this screen provides a complete record of what is in the cookie, allowing the user to make an informed decision about whether or not to accept it. As with Netscape Navigator, however, the user must interact with this screen for each and every cookie unless he or she enlists third-party software to assist with the task.

Microsoft Internet Explorer 4 does not place cookies in a single cookie file as Netscape Navigator 4 does. Instead it produces a separate file for each cookie. These cookie files are typically stored in the "Temporary Internet Files" subdirectory of the Windows directory. Unlike the Netscape Navigator cookie file, these files are not simply plain text. By double-clicking on them and ignoring warning messages, it is possible to look at their contents, but they are hard to decipher. The best way to view them is with a cookie management tool.

Cookie Management Tools

If you want to manage and control cookies, having to stop and deal with a warning box for each and every cookie is burdensome. As already noted, some sites

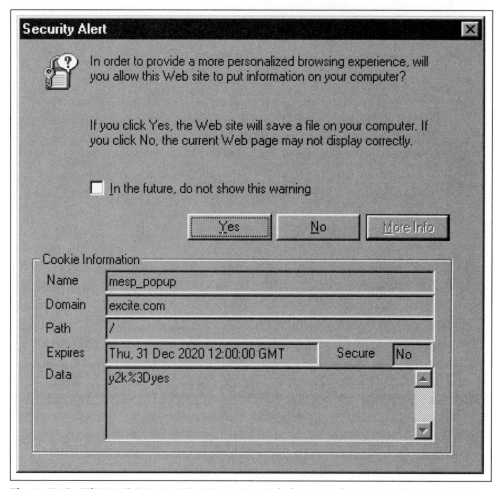

Figure 7–6. Microsoft Internet Explorer 4 cookie information screen (©1999 Microsoft Corporation)

don't easily take no for an answer and persist in trying to send the same cookie over and over, requiring a separate rejection for each attempt.

There are a great many inexpensive third-party products that can be used to make cookie management easier. On a recent visit to a site listing software products available for downloading, I found a score of cookie management programs. They ranged in price from free to twenty dollars or so. Let's look at a couple of examples of such products to see what they do. What follows is not an endorsement or review of any particular product or approach. The intent is simply to give you an idea of what is out there and what your visitors might be doing to your cookies.

The simplest cookie programs don't get involved with whether or not the user accepts or rejects cookies but leave that task to the browser. Instead, these products allow the user to periodically clean up the cookies collected on his or her machine. The simplest products take the point of view that no cookie should be persistent and delete them all. This allows a user to accept cookies without inspection, knowing that they will all be removed at some later time. Some users set up such a program to run every time the computer is started up, ensuring that cookies are never around for very long. There is also a web browser, called "Lynx" (**http://lynx.browser.org/**), that is set up to effectively do the same thing, deleting all cookies each time the user exits the browser. From the user's standpoint, such simple products have the disadvantage that they delete useful cookies, such as ones from trusted sites that speed up the process of signing onto the site.

One step up the ladder from the simple "cookie-blaster" products are programs that recognize that sometimes a user wants to keep some cookies. One such product, called "Cookie Cutter," is from Ayecor software (**http://ayecor.com**) and allows the user to mark certain cookies for preservation, deleting all others. The program can be set up to run automatically at scheduled intervals or can, of course, be set up to run when the computer is started up.

A more sophisticated class of cookie management software works in real time with a browser, intercepting and examining cookies for the user. "Cookie Pal," by Kookaburra Software (**http://www.kburra.com**), for example, takes the place of the web browser's cookie warning box. Rather than simply accepting or rejecting the cookie, Cookie Pal offers choices that include accepting a particular cookie, rejecting a particular cookie, always accepting cookies from a domain, and never accepting cookies from a domain. The "always" and "never" options are the interesting ones because they allow the user to build a set of filters, over time, that automatically let through the cookies of interest and reject the ones that the user doesn't want.

From your standpoint, the wide availability of these products underscores the importance of developing a cooperative relationship with visitors, where they understand why you want to set a cookie and why it benefits them. An interesting, proactive approach to addressing user concerns might include not only explaining why accepting your cookies is OK but also pointing the visitor at one of the more sophisticated cookie management products that automatically filter cookies. In that way, your customers could choose to automatically accept your cookies while still inspecting those from less trusted sources.

Privacy Policy

Because they are such a key part of the process of identifying visitors and tracking their activity, cookies are necessarily also a key element in your company's privacy policy. Our investigation of cookies has uncovered a number of facts about them. When pieced together, these facts create a complex picture:

- Cookies are useful and important to the website developer. They are how you turn the disconnected transaction model of the web into transactions that can maintain state and progress forward.
- The visitor does not control what is placed in a cookie. Careless use of cookies on the part of the site developer could indeed compromise the visitor's privacy. Consequently, visitors need to know that websites are both concerned about the visitor's privacy and competent enough to implement those concerns.
- It really is possible to use cookies to collect the information required to construct a much broader picture of a user's behavior. So website visitors do have legitimate cause for concern regarding cookies.
- Informed users certainly do have tools available to enable them to efficiently delete or reject your cookies. If you want visitors to accept your cookies, you need to be prepared to make a good case for their doing so.

The fact that cookies are useful and important while at the same time representing a potential risk to customers means that cookie use and cookie policy should involve management as well as the technical staff. If you choose to use cookies, you should ensure that you have done so in a way that does not compromise your customers' information and your relationship with those customers.

The need for a company to make a case to its customers *in favor of* using cookies, should you decide in favor of such use, is all the more important because others are certainly making a case *against* accepting cookies. Here is the text used by one cookie management program to motivate purchase of a product:

> Every time you go to a new website, your privacy is in jeopardy. Websites collect information about your preferences by placing a Cookie on your PC. This information can later be viewed and analyzed by others. [Product] will clean up these hidden cookies and prevent websites from snooping around on your machine. It comes with a slick user interface that pops up from the system tray. [Product] allows you to specify automatic cookie cleanup, eliminating the need for human intervention. It works with both MS Internet

Explorer and Netscape browsers. Take control of your privacy. Check out [Product] now.

This is pretty provocative copy. It is also inaccurate: Cookies certainly do not allow anybody to begin "snooping around on your machine." The writer has apparently decided, however, that, in fighting the war against cookies, a little propaganda might be excusable.

Although this particular instance of cookie bashing reaches further than most, it does capture the shape of the fear that users can feel about cookies. The result is that if you want to use and rely on cookies, you need to take serious steps toward allaying user fears.

An appropriate place for management to start is with a clearly stated policy on how your company is addressing privacy concerns. This policy needs to reflect actual practice. A good policy matched up with poor practice will catch up with you, typically sooner rather than later. For example, amazon.com made big news late in the summer of 1999 by introducing a new "fun" feature that allowed visitors to see which books were being purchased most frequently by which businesses. One could learn, for example that one of the top selling books at Delta Airlines was *The Pilot's Wife,* a novel about a pilot who secretly lives with two wives and has families in different cities. You could also find out that one of the most frequently purchased books at BP Amoco, a company working through a merger and layoffs at the time, was *Rites of Passage at $100,000+: The Insider's Lifetime Guide to Executive Job-Changing and Faster Career Progress.*

This kind of lapse in sensitivity to customer privacy is bad judgment as well as bad policy. It is hard to understand how Amazon's staff could have arrived at the decision to offer such information. When the idea came up, why didn't someone along the approval chain simply say, "No, that is private information that we have about the companies that we serve. We don't publish it for entertainment value." Part of the answer, it would seem, must be that there was insufficient corporatewide emphasis on the primacy of customer privacy. Nobody was treating customer trust as a key asset that needed to be protected and nurtured—as something that you do not take risks with, period. This is a matter of attitude and shared company belief, not just of policy. Fortunately, policy, when forcefully stated and enforced, can shape attitude and belief.

An excellent first step in developing a privacy policy is a review of the guidelines issued by the Online Privacy Alliance (OPA), a consortium of companies and associations committed to promoting voluntary (as opposed to governmentally

Table 7–1 OPA Privacy Policy Guidelines

1. **Adoption and Implementation of a Privacy Policy**

   An organization engaged in online activities or electronic commerce has a responsibility to adopt and implement a policy for protecting the privacy of individually identifiable information. Organizations should also take steps that foster the adoption and implementation of effective online privacy policies by the organizations with which they interact; e.g., by sharing best practices with business partners.

2. **Notice and Disclosure**

   An organization's privacy policy must be easy to find, read, and understand. The policy must be available prior to or at the time that individually identifiable information is collected or requested.

   The policy must state clearly: what information is being collected; the use of that information; possible third-party distribution of that information; the choices available to an individual regarding collection, use, and distribution of the collected information; a statement of the organization's commitment to data security; and what steps the organization takes to ensure data quality and access.

   The policy should disclose the consequences, if any, of an individual's refusal to provide information. The policy should also include a clear statement of what accountability mechanism the organization uses, including how to contact the organization.

3. **Choice/Consent**

   Individuals must be given the opportunity to exercise choice regarding how individually identifiable information collected from them online may be used when such use is unrelated to the purpose for which the information was collected. At a minimum, individuals should be given the opportunity to opt out of such use.

   Additionally, in the vast majority of circumstances, where there is third-party distribution of individually identifiable information, collected online from the individual, unrelated to the purpose for which it was collected, the individual should be given the opportunity to opt out.

Consent for such use or third-party distribution may also be obtained through technological tools or opt-in.

4. **Data Security**

   Organizations creating, maintaining, using, or disseminating individually identifiable information should take appropriate measures to assure its reliability and should take reasonable precautions to protect it from loss, misuse, or alteration. They should take reasonable steps to assure that third parties to which they transfer such information are aware of these security practices, and that the third parties also take reasonable precautions to protect any transferred information.

5. **Data Quality and Access**

   Organizations creating, maintaining, using, or disseminating individually identifiable information should take reasonable steps to assure that the data are accurate, complete, and timely for the purposes for which they are to be used.

   Organizations should establish appropriate processes or mechanisms so that inaccuracies in material individually identifiable information, such as account or contact information, may be corrected. These processes and mechanisms should be simple and easy to use, and provide assurance that inaccuracies have been corrected. Other procedures to assure data quality may include use of reliable sources and collection methods, reasonable and appropriate consumer access and correction, and protections against accidental or unauthorized alteration.

mandated) web privacy standards. The OPA guidelines (see end-of-chapter reference 1) have just begun to gather strength and importance. Key advertisers, such as Intel and Disney, have started requiring that sites displaying their advertising conform to OPA guidelines. The complete text of the guidelines is reprinted in Table 7–1 since they are a useful starting point for designing your own policy. The key elements are as follows:

- **Adoption of a policy.** You need to have a specific policy.
- **Notice and disclosure.** The policy needs to be posted on the site so that it is easy to find. It must state exactly what information is being collected, how it will be used, who has access to it, and how your company is ensuring the security of the information. It must also explain the consequences of the visitor's choosing not to disclose information or accept cookies.
- **Choice/consent.** The visitor must consent to participate and must be able to choose not to participate.
- **Data security.** Your company must take reasonable steps to ensure that the data are not available to unauthorized parties or misused.
- **Data quality and access.** You must have mechanisms in place to ensure that any personal data are accurate and complete. You should provide mechanisms to enable verification and correction of such data, which may include review by the individual.

This last point, regarding access, is an interesting one because it underscores the serious responsibility that companies take on as they begin to collect data about individual customers. The Federal Trade Commission also has a set of guidelines (see end-of-chapter reference 2) that speak to this issue. They state that "Access is [a] core principle. It refers to an individual's ability both to access data about him or herself—i.e., to view the data in an entity's files—and to contest that data's accuracy and completeness. Both are essential to ensuring that data are accurate and complete."

As we have already seen, unless visitors register and provide personal identifying information, the data collected on websites are typically anonymous, and so questions about access are moot. But when you do have truly personal information, it is only fair to let the customer see it and request changes as necessary. The idea of needing to let the customer see and correct what you have collected brings the privacy matter into focus. If you are uncomfortable in sharing what you know about a customer with that customer, that in itself should make you want to think twice about your practices.

Privacy and Engagement

The OPA guidelines clearly deal with matters that reach far beyond cookies and what you might be doing with them. But if you want users to work with you and accept your cookies, you need to be able to put your cookie use in the broader context of how you will treat the information that you collect about those users. If you are dealing with a relatively small number of visitors who already have a relationship with you, as is the case in some business-to-business web contexts, explaining your use of cookies and establishing trust and confidence are probably easy. But if the users have a less intimate relationship with your company, establishing trust can be a long, slow process.

A recent study by Jupiter Communications, reported on the CNET site (see end-of-chapter reference 3), found that about 64 percent of the web users included in the survey distrust the truth and significance of online privacy policies. The CNET article speculates that this may be because a number of prominent sites post privacy guidelines but then obviously disregard those guidelines. This brings us back to the importance of coupling policies with a companywide attitude that elevates the importance of protecting customers' privacy above other objectives, even when those other objectives involve increased revenues. Customer relationships are a long-term investment.

The slipshod, careless attitude that web companies have taken with regard to protecting the privacy of information in general gives visitors good reason to be cautious about accepting cookies and providing any personal information. Yet, as we will see in the following chapters, engaging customers so that your site adapts to their individual needs is a very important part of building a web business. Without personal information, you cannot build this kind of site.

This problem is not easy to fix. It requires management attention as well as technical competence. The necessary steps are to develop a comprehensive, fair privacy policy, to then live by it, and to continue advertising the fact that your company is deserving of the trust of your customers and business partners. This is not a quick solution. It is therefore a road that you should start down as soon as possible.

Other Approaches to Maintaining State

Cookies are the most commonly used mechanisms for maintaining continuity and context with a customer, allowing you to engage that customer. The use of cookies provides the foundation for most of the higher-level state maintenance capabilities found in web application servers and other web development environments. But what if a visitor will not accept cookies, even after you have explained how you are using them and why he or she should invest some trust in your company and in your site?

The answer, of course, depends on why you needed the cookie in the first place. If the consequence of the cookie rejection is simply that your web activity log is less complete, then no further action is necessary.

But what if the cookie and its ability to maintain the state of a transaction are essential to completing that transaction? In part, the answer emerges from the "Notice and Disclosure" section of the OPA guidelines, which states, "The policy should disclose the consequences, if any, of an individual's refusal to provide information." If the user still rejects the cookie after being told that it will last only as long as the session (question for you—why would you need it any longer?) and that the cookie is necessary to complete the transaction, then it might be reasonable to wonder about the value of this particular customer or visitor. Is this person really a prospective buyer?

However, suppose that even after all of this you still want to find an alternative approach to proceeding with the transaction. Is there any alternative to the use of cookies that allows you to maintain the state of transactions?

Yes, there is. Once again, since our focus here is on supporting business managers rather than technical staff, we will concentrate on identifying the alternative and enumerating its advantages and disadvantages.

As we said in Chapter 6, keeping track of state requires finding a place to store information between page views. This is necessary because the web protocol is set up so that the web server regards each request as a world unto itself, independent of every other request. Cookies solve this problem by using a little bit of storage on the client machine to save the state of the transaction.

Another source of storage space, apart from the client computer, is in the URL itself. In addition to the address for a page, URLs can contain parameters that transmit other information between the web client and the server. We saw an instance of the use of parameters in Chapter 2, when we looked at the referrer entries for a visitor coming in from a search engine. Here is what that entry looked like:

```
http://www.altavista.com/cgi-bin/query?pg=q&kl=
    XX&q=%22personalization+and+customization%22 ->/
    members/NEPs/BayNetworks.htm
```

The URL in this entry extends from "http" to the second "%22." Everything after the question mark is parameter information. This information is ignored by the web server as it tries to find the right page to deliver or the right script to execute. The server effectively strips off the parameter information, making it available to the script for whatever purpose that the script might have. In the case of a search engine, the script fires off a query against the retrieval system index. In the case of a transaction, the parameters can be used to maintain state. They could, for example, hold information about the contents of a shopping cart, serving as an alternative to the use of cookies.

There are some disadvantages to using storage in a URL rather than in a cookie. The most obvious one is that a URL is not persistent across sessions. So, unlike a cookie, URL parameters cannot help you recognize and provide special attention to returning customers. (On the other hand, from the standpoint of a visitor nervous about privacy, this lack of persistence might be a big advantage.) Another problem, perhaps more serious because it gets in the way of using URL parameters even in temporary applications such as shopping carts, is that parameter-based applications can be fragile if a user begins to move backward in a transaction or browses around before completing the sale. If a user clicks on the "Back" button, the parameters are suddenly gone, and the shopping cart is empty, which is perhaps not what the customer actually wanted.

There are yet other alternatives, such as asking the user to log in with a username and password and then relying on user identification mechanisms supplied within HTTP. This alternative is not really very practical, however: If the visitor is skittish about letting you set a cookie, it is very unlikely that he or she will give you identifying information required to set up a login and password.

The bottom line is that cookies are, by far, the most flexible tool available to you as you try to develop more sophisticated ways of interacting with customers and business partners. To the extent that visitors resist the use of cookies, your best bet is to assure them that you are using cookies and the information that you collect in responsible ways, so that you can build trust over time. This requires that you consider carefully just why you need cookies and just what you intend to do with visitor information and then that you put policies and training in place to ensure that your entire company does not unwittingly breach the trust and confidence that you are working so hard to establish.

Summary

Providing individual, personal attention to your customers is an important ingredient of success in web business—an ingredient that we will explore in detail in subsequent chapters of this book. You cannot provide individual, personal attention to customers unless you understand their needs and preferences, and you cannot understand their needs and preferences unless they trust your company enough to provide them to you. The bottom line is that getting your customers to trust you is an absolutely essential requirement for success in web business.

Collecting and using customer information is an area in which there is potential for damaging trust. The key to success in this area involves recognition that the exchange of information is, in fact, a trade. The customer must receive benefit in return for the information that he or she provides. As the sensitivity and personal nature of the information increases, so must the value that the customer receives. Making this trade-off explicit, and helping customers to understand just what you are doing are important ingredients of success. Another key part of building trust and exchanging value for information involves recognizing that the relationship with the customer grows over time, moving from simple requests for general information to more complete engagement.

Cookies tend to be a central part of this negotiation with customers since they involve storing data on the customer's machine and are a primary mechanism used to identify and track customers. Consequently, the decision about how and why to use cookies is not one that should just be left to the technical staff. Management should be involved and should drive such decisions on the basis of business objectives and concern for customer relations.

Customers have a number of tools available to them to evaluate and filter cookies. One approach to building engagement is to help customers become more familiar with such tools so that they can easily accept cookies from sites that they trust (which would presumably include your site).

Cookies should be treated as a key element within your company's overall approach to privacy and your care of the information entrusted to you by your customers. A key objective should be to develop a companywide attitude that treats the information that customers and visitors allow you to collect as an asset that is not to be compromised. The goal is to establish a corporatewide habit of asking whether any decision or promotional campaign might in some way put customer privacy at risk.

A key component of a program to create awareness of the importance of guarding customer information and privacy is the articulation of an aggressive privacy policy. The policy should be posted on your website where it is easy to find and should include provisions ensuring that visitors understand what they are disclosing and why. They should have the option not to participate in an exchange of information with your company and should understand the consequences of not participating. The policy should also ensure that any personal data is correct and secure and should provide customers with a way to review and verify the data.

Customer concerns about cookies naturally raise the question of whether there are alternatives to the use of cookies to maintain the state of an interaction. It is possible to use storage space within the URL to maintain state, but this approach has significant disadvantages relative to the use of cookies. The best approach involves clear articulation of why you use cookies, of the benefits to the customer, and of how you use and protect the information that you collect.

Key Ideas

- Information about customer preferences and requirements is a necessary ingredient to personalized engagement. Obtaining such information requires a trade of benefit for information with your customers. Setting up the terms of this trade so that your customers understand them is a key step toward customer engagement.
- Cookies are both part of collecting the information and an important element of the overall program to build trust.
- There are a number of tools and approaches for managing cookies from the customer side. You can incorporate such tools as part of your program to engage customers and to ensure that they can easily exchange information with trusted businesses.
- Creation of an effective privacy policy is important because it can help with the all-important matter of creating a corporate culture that values and protects customer information.
- Cookies are the preferred tool for maintaining state. Other approaches are available. If you have problems with cookie acceptance, however, you should work on better policies and trust rather than merely on providing a substitute mechanism.

References in This Chapter

1. The Online Privacy Alliance (OPA) guidelines, along with other useful information, are available at **http://www.privacyalliance.org/**.
2. The Federal Trade Commission's Fair Information Practice Principles are available at **http://www.ftc.gov/reports/privacy3/fairinfo.htm#Fair Information Practice Principles**.
3. The CNET article on privacy policies, which cites the Jupiter study, is "Report: Half of Net Users Mistrust Sites," by Sandeep Junnarkar (CNET, August 17, 1999: **http://www.news.com/News/Item/0,4,40597,00.html**).

Further Reading

Simon St. Laurent's *Cookies* (McGraw-Hill, 1998), which was referenced in Chapter 6, is relevant to the material covered in this chapter as well. As mentioned, it complements the treatment here with an approach aimed at the website developer.

The Federal Trade Commission's June 1998 report to Congress is an excellent overview of privacy issues and practice. It is available online at **http://www.ftc.gov/reports/privacy3/toc.htm**.

There are a growing number of websites that deal exclusively with privacy issues. Two of the most prominent ones are the Electronic Frontier Foundation at **http://www.eff.org** and Junkbusters at **http://www.junkbusters.com**. They both contain current news about privacy issues, initiatives, and violations, as well as advice about protecting privacy. Junkbusters includes a paper titled "How Web Servers' Cookies Threaten Your Privacy" (**http://www.junkbusters.com/ht/en/cookies.html**) that argues strongly against accepting cookies. If you want to use cookies to maintain state and serve other useful functions, understanding these arguments is essential.

Finally, Junkbusters maintains an exhaustive, continually updated list of online articles, print articles, books, and professional papers dealing with a wide range of privacy issues. It is available at **http://www.junkbusters.com/ht/en/links.html**. Although this list is large, it is annotated, which makes using it manageable. It is a valuable resource for anyone looking for tools, viewpoints, and information on electronic privacy.

CHAPTER EIGHT

Personalization: Using Customer Data

Objectives of This Chapter

- Introduce ways to move from collecting data about individual customers to using the data to strengthen the relationship with your customers, creating market advantage for your business.
- Show how personalization can be just as important in business-to-business settings as when you are selling directly to the end customer.
- Provide a real-life example of how personalization can help a web business grow—an example that we can use as we look at personalization more closely.

Putting Customer Data to Work

Over the next few chapters, we will show you how to use data about individual customers to connect your business to their particular needs. In so doing, you will tie your customers more tightly to your business.

This is a new layer of construction on the edifice that we have built over the preceding chapters. Taking a brief high-level look at the concepts and techniques that we have developed in the preceding chapters is useful at this point since the earlier work is an important foundation for what we are about to build next.

We began by looking at the handful of important high-level questions that you need to be able to answer about your web business. These questions are important because they provide you with critical and basic insight into how people are using your business and on how they value it. We saw that, on the web, your business does not always look the same as it does when you are dealing with customers face to face. The first step in customer engagement is getting a clear picture of how the customer sees you.

We saw that the information that is collected in log files is able to provide answers to many of these larger questions. We also found that the log file data, though useful for providing aggregate information about customers, tells us very little about particular customers. This led to a careful discussion of cookies, which can help you recognize individual customers during a session on your website and as they return. Cookies help you move from having a general picture of your customers to having a view of each separate customer.

Success in web business depends on balancing these two different viewpoints, responding both to the general needs and direction of the business and to the needs and preferences of individual customers. Is there some way to use your website to meet each customer's needs while at the same time meeting the different needs of other customers? This is the question that we will explore in the next few chapters. It is the concern that underlies web business efforts to personalize websites.

Personalize or Perish?

Recently, I received a glossy folder offering me the choice to "personalize or perish." As if running a web business were not complicated enough, the four companies behind this promotional campaign have discovered yet another way to die on the Internet.

Opening up the folder, I learned: "Just one click away, your fiercest competitors are satisfying Web visitors with personalization technology. Your online customers have come to expect this level of service. So has your CEO." Uh-oh, everyone else but me is already in on the game, which leads to the question, Are you up to speed on the new e-marketing mandate?

This is a lot like the advertising copy for cookie management software that we looked at in Chapter 7. What is it about the Internet that compels companies to scare you into action rather than showing you how you can benefit?

Part of what is going on here is that the companies selling personalization products and services are using the word *personalization* in two ways. Sorting out the two uses, like separating the sizzle from the steak, is critical for you as a buyer.

Most people agree that a good web business personalizes its relationships with customers and partners. Certainly, as one looks at the changes in web business over the past three or four years, it is clear that most businesses started out by using the web as a cheap, fast broadcast publishing medium. Early websites were essentially a high-tech, low-resolution way to deliver marketing literature. Over the past few years, such "brochureware" has evolved into websites focused on customer interaction. Personalizing interaction is a good thing. It is the potential for one-to-one interaction that makes Internet business so potentially valuable and different. Personalization, when discussed in this way, is a very general and fuzzy concept. It is like talking about freedom. There is no doubt that it exists, and no doubt that it is a good thing. It's the sizzle.

Personalization as fuzzy concept, like motherhood, freedom, and sizzle, is not something that can be bought and sold by itself. The buying and the selling involve products and services. The second sense of personalization revolves around what the glossy direct-mail piece called "personalization technology." It is clearly advantageous for a vendor to try to connect the two senses of the word: "Personalization is the key to the Internet, and, hey, we are just the folks to sell you some."

Blurring the two senses of the word together by having personalization as a key feature of the web and also as a product or technology makes the subject confusing for anyone trying to run a web business. Personalizing your interaction with customers and suppliers can involve many tools and technologies. Personalization can be applied in a wide variety of circumstances for an equally broad array of purposes. In this chapter and the ones that follow, we will help you sort out the different approaches to using personalized information delivery and will help you outline a program to make increasingly sophisticated use of personalization in your web business over time. We begin with an example of personalization that works.

A Personalization Success Story

There is a tendency to associate personalization with consumer businesses. When asked for an example of personalization on the web, many people think of going to a site like Amazon and receiving recommendations for books and CDs based on their past purchases. Although such business-to-consumer applications of personalization are highly visible and often very successful, it is frequently in the business-to-business setting that personalization pays off most directly and quickly. Time is money for business users, and personalization can save time. Let's look at an example.

National Semiconductor makes its money by selling chips, millions of them, that are embedded in electronics systems of all kinds. It turns out that one of the keys to selling chips is to get them in front of the hardware engineers who design electronic products and who specify the components to be used in those products. If a company can succeed in getting engineers to order sample quantities of chips and to then use those chips in the early prototypes for products, there is a very good chance that there will eventually be large orders for manufacturing quantities of the chips as the products go into production.

Electronics engineers were an ideal target audience for early web business applications. They had computers early and were comfortable with using technology. They also have information-intensive jobs: Keeping up with the rapid pace of electronics technology development so that a design uses the most cost-effective components is demanding work. Finally, sending sample components to engineers is a nearly perfect early e-commerce application. There is no need to be concerned about payment mechanisms since the samples are free. At the same time, the sample chips are valuable and yet very small and light. The high value-to-weight ratio is important in web applications because the goods need to be shipped out to the customer.

In fact, putting up catalogs of components for hardware engineers was such a great and obvious idea that nearly every semiconductor manufacturer and component supplier was doing it. National's challenge, then, was not simply to get a components catalog up and running. It needed, instead, to create a web business that was somehow different and more attractive for the target audience. It needed to find a way to use its website to create competitive advantage, drawing an increasing number of hardware design engineers to the site and to National's products.

Succeeding at this goal required a deeper understanding of the hardware engineer's needs and problems. What is it about finding and selecting components for new products that is particularly difficult and unworkable? Which of these problems might be addressed through an Internet business? To answer these questions, National went out and talked with a great many hardware engineers, asking them just how they went about keeping track of new products and technologies and how they then used this information in designing a product.

The picture that emerged from the research was complex, but the general shape of the process seemed to be that the engineers regularly paged through technical journals and industry trade magazines. They clipped out articles and advertisements and tossed them in a file drawer. When a new design project started up, out came the clippings. The designer would sort them into piles, keying information into spreadsheets and other tools to make it easier to compare alternatives and evaluate options. He or she would then go to the manufacturers' websites and download specifications. Eventually, the designer would order samples of the components that looked most useful and promising. The things that the hardware designer did not like about this process were that it was hit-and-miss, potentially incomplete, and took a lot of time.

The challenge for National, then, was to find a way to use the web to serve as some kind of electronic file drawer that would automatically fill up with clippings about National's products. It was clear that this would involve more than just putting the parts catalog online. The system would need to

- Provide personalized workspaces—virtual file drawers—for every customer.
- Replicate the function of sorting through the piles of clippings to get a sense of what is available and possible. The interviews showed that designers do not move in a straight line toward some specific part with particular characteristics. Instead, they consider families of related parts as they weigh design alternatives.
- Help the designers keep up to date on current information—and on the *right* information. If possible, National needed to find some way to use personalization to automatically fill the file drawers with the information that customers needed.

National approached these requirements with an array of personalization features, ranging from simple registration and purchase histories for occasional customers to full-blown, private extranet sites for active corporate accounts. In each case, from simplest to most complex, the goal is to help the buyer save time and therefore money.

As an example of how personalization translates into time savings, registered customers have the ability to create a custom home page that becomes their personal entry point to the National website. National gives these customers the tools to use this home page as the collecting point for product status and bulletins on up to 20 different National products. The personal home page becomes the developer's virtual file drawer, and the bulletin service ensures that the drawer always contains the latest news about the products in which the customer is most interested. This kind of personalization has reduced the number of screen views per transaction on the National site from 7 in 1995, down to 4 in 1996, to 2.7 in 1997, and to 2.2 by the start of 1999. Allowing customers to create their own personal sites that contain only the information that they need turns into real time savings for them.

National has also created more than 100 private websites for OEM customers (original equipment manufacturers) and other large corporate buyers. Corporate customers can use these password-protected private sites to create and store multiple design projects, each with its own bill of materials. National's site actually becomes part of the corporate buyer's planning and tracking mechanisms. These private account pages provide customers with a window into National's internal systems. They can look up their corporate contracts with National, keep track of inventory, and can monitor order availability of the parts they need for their designs. OEM customers can even see preliminary data sheets for products that are not yet shipping and can track the status of National's product development process.

With all of this investment in personalization and the effort to make the site easier to use, National has also invested in systems that monitor site performance. Using a combination of systems, National tracks both overall site usage statistics and more detailed information, such as just how registered users navigate the site. Because the focus of the personalization effort is to make the site easier to use, National closely monitors the number of page views required to reach a transaction. They also look to see what kinds of activities typically lead to transactions and work to increase the width of the "buying funnel," thus turning more visitors into customers.

How is all of this working? In our own conversations with design engineers, we found that they like the National site because it fits closely with the way they do their work. They compare it favorably with other sites that take the manufacturer's catalog as the organizing principle rather than starting from the designer's needs and work process.

Learning by Example

National Semiconductor's work with personalization is interesting not only because it shows that personalization can be an important part of a business-to-business website but also because it contains a number of important lessons about personalization.

The Customer at the Center

Perhaps the most important thing about personalization on the National site is that the customer benefits directly. This lesson is so simple and obvious that it is easy to overlook. Often a company will put so much energy into thinking about what it wants from personalization—increased sales of its primary product, cross-selling, more information about customers, and so on—that it forgets that customers won't play unless there is something in it for them, too. On National's site, personalization is focused on saving the customer time. Now, it so happens that saving time for the customer makes it easier for the customer to order samples—a connection that is never far from National's consciousness. The primary focus, however, is on the customer's problem. National wins when the customer wins.

Because there is clear benefit to the customer, National is able to ask the customer directly for information that helps personalize the site: What kinds of products are you interested in? What information do you want us to keep updated on your home page? Rather than having to deduce information about customers, National can just ask them for it. The second lesson from National's experience, then, is that the most cost-effective way to gather the customer profiles required to support personalization is also often the most direct—have the customer tell you. This capability, of course, assumes that you have taken care of the first matter of providing clear customer benefit.

A third observation about National's personalization program is that customers are, to a great degree, in control of how much personalization they receive and how much information they divulge. This is an important part of ensuring that customers are comfortable with the system. In a sense, the amount of personalization is itself personalized.

The final observation about building personalization around the customer is also so simple and obvious that it, too, would be easy to overlook. National did not try to learn everything that it needed to know about customers just through the collection of website data. Instead, National went out and talked to customers. It commissioned surveys of customer needs and preferences. Just because you are a web business, there is no need to limit yourself only to information that you can get through your website.

Beyond Customer Choice

As critical as the customer's role is in shaping the style and content of personalization at National, not everything on the National site is driven by the customer. The customer makes choices, but so does National. The personalized web experience for any customer is an intersection of the customer's interests and National's interests.

National's input into the personalization mechanism comes in the form of deciding which information to deliver and which new products to emphasize. Given an outline of a particular customer's requirements and focus, National creates a personalized home page containing information that is likely to be of interest to that customer. The customer gets to say which kinds of products he or she is interested in; National gets to decide what to publish in response to those expressions of interest.

National regards the details of just how it matches products to customer interests as confidential information since it is a big part of the company's use of personalization as a competitive tool. In general, however, there are two ways to automate personalized publishing. The first is to use some kind of "recommendation engine" to observe customer buying patterns and preferences and then to make new recommendations to a customer based on the patterns of other customers. The second is to have marketers and product managers set up specific rules that can be used to automatically deliver particular information in response to specific requests or user actions. For example, when National introduces a new, higher-performance component, the product marketer can create a rule that tells the system to offer the new component as an alternative whenever a customer is considering one of the older, lower-performance versions of the product. National has found that customers don't mind receiving such up-sell and cross-sell information as long as it is reasonably related to the work that they are doing.

Lessons from National

There is much to be learned from National's experiences with personalization. Perhaps the simplest and most important lesson is that personalization should be an important component of any business-to-business website. The lifetime value of a business-to-business customer is typically many times that of a business-to-consumer customer. Given the importance of creating and maintaining such high-value relationships, it makes sense to provide business customers with a personalized site that saves them time and that ties them to your company.

Beyond underscoring the importance and utility of personalization, National's example also provides us with important insights about how to get the job done. Perhaps the central lesson is that personalization must benefit the customer. You, of course, are interested in personalization because of what it might do for you in terms of increased sales, but none of that will happen unless the personalization provides clear value to the people using your site. In many business settings, as for National, the chief benefit of personalization for the customer is time savings.

Tied to this focus on customer benefit is the requirement that the customer needs to have some control over the nature, content, and degree of personalization. Getting the customer involved helps you, too: You can ask directly for customer profile information and interests rather than having to develop profiles by more indirect means.

Personalization is not a one-way street but is, instead, an interaction that converges in the direction of better understanding and better service. The customer has input into the process, and so do you. In many cases, as with National, the input from the company's side consists of deciding what promotions, new products, and other information to provide to the customer in response to his or her requests and purchases. If the additional information passes the test of providing real utility for the customer, it can then help you broaden your relationship with that customer, selling other products or higher-value products in response to customer requests.

National's experience with personalization shows that it can be a key part of building a high-performance web business. Personalized information delivery has helped National avoid being just another electronics component website. Instead, National's website has emerged as a preferred first source for information and components used in the design process. The personalized interaction with customers has turned into an electronic conversation that not only delivers design and product information to customers but also provides National with important knowledge about the customers and insights into their needs. The site generates leads for the National sales force and, even better, shows salespeople which customers have ordered which sample parts. It also provides National with forecast information relating to production demand and with information about trends and requirements that can be used to drive new product development.

The Three Basic Approaches to Personalization

One problem consistently faced by web business managers who want to understand and apply personalization technologies is that there are so many different tools and approaches. This makes it hard to sort out the alternatives. We have found that it is useful to begin by grouping the different personalization tools and approaches into three categories, based on just who or what is in control of the personalization process. The three categories are

1. Personalization that the customer controls.
2. Products and technologies that use the computer to control personalization.
3. Approaches that put the marketer in control.

Over the next chapters, we will look at the kinds of products and techniques that are collected in each of these categories. This should help you sort things out so that you can see which products and techniques compete with one another and which ones can be used together in a complementary way to offer richer personalization. Once we have the pieces labeled and laid out, we will conclude with some suggestions about how to assemble them, helping you think through the process of preparing the foundation for personalized interactions and showing you how to approach personalization in stages.

Summary

In this chapter, we began to turn our focus to the use of website and customer data to connect your business directly with the needs of individual customers. The popular general term for such connection is *personalization*.

The term is by now a full-fledged buzzword. As such, it confuses a good idea—that of connecting to the customer—with a rapidly expanding set of technologies and product offers that claim to enable the connection. One of our goals over the next few chapters will be to provide you with enough understanding of the principles behind personalization and web customer engagement to enable you to make reasoned, considered judgments about the different offers.

The primary focus in this chapter is on introducing a useful example of a web business that is making effective use of personalization. We focused on National Semiconductor because personalization is critical to the success of its web business, because it is using the personalization in a number of different ways, because it is succeeding in using personalization effectively, and because it is using personalization to sell to other businesses. This last point is important because there is a general misconception that personalization is important only in selling to consumers.

The relatively high lifetime value of a customer in a business-to-business setting suggests that just the opposite should be true. As illustrated by National Semiconductor, time savings through efficient interaction with a website can be a major focus for business buyers. A site that can make a job easier and faster can help a company build market share. Personalization of the site for each customer, setting it up to reflect individual customer needs and preferences upon entry to the site, is a key component of creating that kind of speed and ease of use.

The National Semiconductor example also illustrates the important fact that meaningful personalization requires the customer's permission and participation. At the most fundamental level, this permission involves accepting a cookie. Beyond that, it means having the customer provide profile information and other expressions of preferences and needs so that it is, in fact, possible to personalize the site for that customer. The requirement for active customer participation leads to another important requirement for successful personalization: The personalization must provide real benefit to the customer. It cannot just be a way for you to sell more; customers need to be able to clearly see what is in it for them.

An important outcome of collecting the information required to provide customers with a personalized site is that you end up knowing much more about your customers. National has been able to use its personalized interactions with customers to provide important information to its sales, product development, and production planning operations.

Key Ideas

- Personalization is a set of approaches and techniques for engaging the customer more directly. It is not a single product or technology, but a combination of activities that needs to make sense for your business and your customers.
- Websites providing business-to-business information and products are particularly well suited to investments in personalization because the high value of each customer relationship makes it easy to justify the expenditure on acquiring and keeping that customer.
- Personalization must involve the customer if it is to reflect the customer's needs and preferences in any detail.
- There needs to be clear benefit to the customer in order to support the personalization.
- One of the very useful benefits of implementing personalization is that it becomes an excellent way for you to learn more about your customers.

Further Reading

A great deal has been written about the promise of personalization on the Internet. Much of it tends toward breathless prose that describes the vast dimensions of a grand new future. It reminds me of the predictions about "electricity too cheap to meter" back when pundits first discovered the "peaceful atom." In other words, much of this writing, though stirring, will not help you build your web business.

The One to One Future, by Don Peppers and Martha Rogers, is by now one of the classic texts in the area of building market share through customer-centered marketing. Peppers and Rogers, to their credit, understood the impact of one-to-one marketing in 1993, before the Internet was a significant part of anyone's marketing landscape. You should be familiar with the concepts and concerns outlined in this book.

If Peppers and Rogers are a good resource to explore some of the big ideas surrounding personalization, then Jim Sterne's *Customer Service on the Internet* gets down to the nuts and bolts. This book collects stories and examples from many companies that are using the Internet to interact more closely with customers. All the references to different websites and businesses can, at times, make it difficult to extract the view of the forest from all of these trees. Nonetheless, the book is a useful source of ideas about how to integrate your website with e-mail and with the rest of your customer service operation to connect more closely to customers.

CHAPTER NINE

Responding to the Customer

Objectives of This Chapter

- Put in place the foundation for thinking about personalization and customization in a deliberate, analytical way that is tied to the goals of your business.
- Look at the important things that you can learn by asking customers directly.
- Show how the data from customers is one of several parts of a personalization system.
- Identify the different ways that you can personalize your site for customers, based on information they give you.
- Provide approaches to calculating the costs and benefits of personalization.
- Explore dynamic information delivery so that you have a way to deliver the personalized information.
- Begin looking at customer segmentation—a topic explored in more detail in Chapter 10.

Personalization Controlled by the Customer

National Semiconductor's experiences show the importance of engaging the customer directly in the personalization process. Instead of just studying log files and other data for clues about what the customer wants and needs, National asks customers directly. The customer provides critically important input into the personalization activity and has significant control over the process.

Understanding the advantages of engaging customers directly is easier if we step back and think about the entire personalization process. Figure 9–1 provides a simple diagram of a personalization system. Actually, as we will find later, this diagram is too simple. We will need to add to it in subsequent chapters. But, for now, it helps us focus on the key inputs to the process.

One input is information about the needs of different customer *groups*. The groups are important because websites are never infinitely customizable for each user. You make some decisions up front about the general personalization options that you will make available, and then the personalization has to work within these options. Such up-front decisions are typically informed by your picture of the different groups that you serve.

An example will help make this matter of groups easier to understand. National Semiconductor provides customers with the choice of newsletters and product bulletins. Successful design and creation of the newsletters depend on understanding the audience or "group" of readers that share interest in a particular

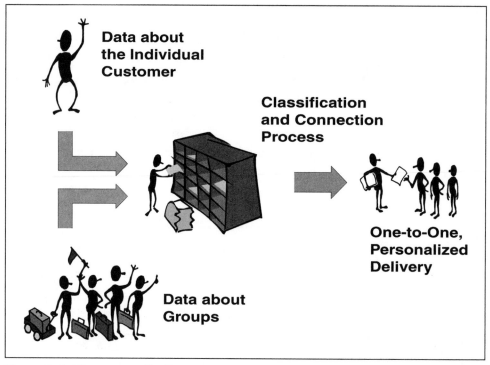

Figure 9–1 The personalization process

topic. As we will see later, this process of deciding on the makeup and interests of the different groups can be done by gut feel, by automated processes, or as a result of careful statistical market segmentation. One way or another, you define some groups and then identify the content or services in which the group is most interested.

The other input in Figure 9–1 is information about each *individual customer*. When a particular customer comes to the site, you match the information about him or her with the information about the groups, deciding where he or she best fits. These decisions might be very straightforward, as when a customer directly identifies the special-interest group to which he or she wants to subscribe. The decisions can also be complicated and probabilistic, determining group affiliation algorithmically. In any case, when you match the customer to the group, then you can send that individual the content that is of interest to that group.

As with any attempt to simplify a system in order to explain it, there are exceptions and details that we are leaving out here. We will fill them in later. The key points, for the moment, are that you need good information about individuals, information about the makeup and interests of groups, and a way to connect the two and send out the information. Let's begin by looking at what the individual customer can tell you about himself or herself.

First Things First: Identifying the Customer

Providing useful personalization for your customers requires knowing who they are. This is true in a broad sense, of course, since you need to know about their preferences and interests. But it is also true in the most fundamental sense: You need to be able to recognize them as who they are when they return to your site. Personalization implies having an identity.

From the discussions in earlier chapters, we know that IP addresses and other data automatically captured by the web server and maintained in log files are not unique and reliable enough to allow you to recognize customers. Consequently, support for personalization requires, at the very least, setting a cookie on the visitor's machine. A unique identifier placed in the cookie allows you to recognize each particular machine and web browser combination on return visits.

A machine and web browser combination is not, of course, the same as a person. More than one person might use a particular computer, and each person might use more than one machine. Consequently, most sites offering personalization capabilities go beyond just setting a cookie (although they do that, too), requiring visitors to register if they want personalized service. Registration typically involves providing a login name and password. The registration form might also ask for name, address, and other descriptive information. Although such information is not, strictly speaking, required in order to recognize a returning customer, it is certainly nice to have. The one very useful identifier, beyond login and password, is the visitor's e-mail address since this gives you another channel for communicating with your visitor. It is easy to ensure that the e-mail address is correct rather than "made up." Just make completion of the registration process dependent on the customer's entry of a code sequence that is sent to him or her via e-mail.

Registration information—name, password, e-mail address, and so on—is typically stored in a database coupled to the web server. The database can also be used to keep track of other information about the customer as you collect it. Such information might include purchase history, frequency of visits, parts of your site visited, and so on.

As in all interactions with your website visitors and customers, asking them to register is usefully thought of as a trade. They need to get something in return for giving you something. In this case, it should be an easy trade, assuming that you are designing the personalization so that it provides real value to the customer in terms of time savings, ease of use, or new functionality. To get these benefits, visitors need to give you some information about themselves. We sometimes encounter sites that need to offer T-shirts, caps, or other inducements to get visitors to register. While we acknowledge that such promotions might be necessary in circumstances where the benefits of personalization are not immediately obvious—they sometimes have to be experienced to be appreciated—we view the need for such promotions as a sign of potential difficulty to come. You are on much stronger ground if the personalization is clearly, intrinsically valuable. Registration is the first step toward creating a relationship with your customers.

Profiles

Giving customers a way to customize the operation of your site to suit their needs and preferences is among the simplest and most rewarding ways to provide website personalization. It is mutually rewarding because the customers get value from personalization that they can control completely, and you get information directly from customers about what they like and what they need.

At a high level, the mechanism is simple. The customers provide you with information about their needs and interests, and you use that information to drive automated systems that determine what you deliver and how you deliver it. In practice, there are many different ways to implement this, and there are several different focuses for the profiling.

Profiles for Content

The most common, and often the most useful, focus is on the content delivered to the customer. As we saw earlier, National Semiconductor allows registered visitors to choose from up to 20 products for which they will receive bulletins about new developments, ensuring that the content on any registered visitor's private National home page is only the content that the visitor needs and wants. Similarly, the *Wall Street Journal Interactive Edition* allows subscribers to set up a "Personal Journal" that pulls out the articles of particular interest to that customer, every day, and creates a kind of private edition of the newspaper.

Extracting content in response to profile information happens in two ways in the Personal Journal, illustrating both of the typical approaches to this task. One way of finding the right content depends on use of a full-text retrieval engine that extracts and indexes the words in each article. Visitors, in constructing their profiles, enter particular words or phrases related to the content that they want to receive. Each time a visitor asks for his or her personal page, the system uses the retrieval engine to identify the recent articles containing the desired words or phrases.

The second approach to matching the profile to content depends on classification of the content. The subscriber identifies the categories of information of interest, selecting from a list. In the *Wall Street Journal*'s case, the classifications are in terms of particular columns and regular features. For example, a subscriber can create a Personal Journal that always contains the day's "Personal Technology" article and editorials.

Profiles for Presentation

Content is not the only aspect of your website that can be personalized through use of profiles. It is also possible, and usually fairly easy, to give the visitor some control over the appearance and format of the information being delivered. Does the user prefer to see a list of product names and short, one-line descriptions, or does he or she want to be able to review products by looking at a full specification sheet, working page by page? Does the user prefer to see a picture of each product next to the listing in a catalog, or would he or she rather work from a text list? Particularly in business-to-business settings, where it is important to make the use of the site efficient for each user, providing such formatting and presentation options can sometimes add real value for customers.

Profiles for Business Rules

Perhaps the most far-reaching kinds of profile building involve customizing a site for a whole company. In business-to-business commerce, the customer is often a group of many different people working for a single company. The different employees working for the corporate customer may have different individual needs and often will have different levels of authority. If you are selling, say, maintenance, repair, and operating (MRO) supplies to the customer, it will probably be the case that some of the customer's employees can only request purchases and that those purchases need to be approved by someone else in the company before the order is complete. Other employees may be able to order directly but only up to a certain spending limit or within certain categories of supplies. Other, more senior managers not only may be able to order anything in the list but also may be able to add and remove things from the list. It may also be that each of your customers has negotiated different contracts with different levels of discounts on supplies so that each corporate customer ends up seeing what is essentially a personalized catalog with contents and pricing that are unique to that customer. This is the kind of capability provided by software vendors such as Ariba, Commerce One, and Broadvision.

The profile in this case applies to a whole company. It includes not only specifications about which content to show and how to display it but also a description of the business logic required by that customer. In a sense, the profile reflects the internal processes used by your customer. You end up creating a kind of multilevel profiling system, with profiles for individual employees tied together in a framework that reflects the levels of authority and the approval processes established within the client corporation.

The effect of this system is that each corporate customer gets its own private version of your website. How you actually implement this varies, depending on how many different customers you are supporting and on how divergent and unique their needs are. If you are supporting a relatively small number of customers (a dozen or so), you might want to create a separate extranet for each customer, carving off a unique storage area on your site and using it for a particular customer. Only the customers and you have access to the particular subdirectories on the site dedicated to information that you share with them and that they share with you. This last aspect is important: The extranet can be opened up so that the customer, too, can publish information. You might, for example, choose to support a discussion forum so that the client can get product support and answers to questions in a private setting where those questions are seen only by people in the client's company and yours. Or the client might provide you with plans and specifications for new products, along with production schedule information, so that you can coordinate your shipping schedule with that client's needs.

Personalization and Customization

As we begin talking about extranets, private discussion forums, and other special services, it is useful to try to distinguish between the terms *personalization* and *customization*. You will hear both terms used in discussions about websites, and you will hear each term used differently by different speakers. An authoritative definition that distinguishes neatly between the terms and that everyone would agree on is probably impossible. However, there is a generally accepted sense that personalization and customization represent two ends of a spectrum of ways to serve customers.

When you get to the point where you are creating a separate extranet and supporting private discussions for a customer, you are providing what most people would call a "customized" site: It is a site tailored to just that customer and contains information seen only by that customer. It is an expensive approach, but one that can be easily justified for important enough customers. We saw that National Semiconductor sets up customized extranets for manufacturers making heavy use of National's products, providing them with production and logistics information that can tie directly into each customer's manufacturing process. That is customization.

To the extent that you are providing each customer with the same basic information (e.g., items from your catalog) but are merely offering that information in a way that is tailored to customer needs or preferences, most people would say that you are "personalizing" that information. You are not delivering custom content and services, but you are personalizing the common content so that it is easier for the customer to use it.

There is no "right" answer, for all customers and situations, to the question of whether you should provide customization or personalization. The answer depends on weighing the costs against the benefits, which is the problem that we look at next.

A quick note on our use of the terms in this and in the following chapters: We will use *personalization* as a global term that embraces the spectrum of options from providing a few simple options at the one end to providing fully customized extranets on the other. Our focus is primarily on giving you a good picture of the range of options available to you, along with a framework that allows you to choose the appropriate tools for your business needs.

Calculating Costs and Benefits of Personalization

One of the valuable side effects of looking at customization and personalization as different ends of the cost-and-complexity spectrum is that it helps bring questions of costs and benefits into focus. Obviously, both approaches can have value. Just as obviously, as you move closer to the customization end of the continuum, the process is more expensive. What would make that additional expense worthwhile? There are two possible answers to this question:

1. **Increases in the net revenues that you reasonably expect to receive from a customer over the life of your relationship.** This is a hard thing to calculate precisely, but just working to make the estimates can show you a lot. What is the average length of a relationship with a customer, and how much business do you do over that lifetime? If there is essentially no customer relationship (e.g., you are selling a commodity where price is the biggest factor in sales), you should look with a skeptical eye at expensive personalization work. On the other hand, if your buyers are like the hardware engineers at National Semiconductor or if you are a consulting business serving just a few customers, the cost of extensive personalization and even customization may be easy to justify. The expenditures may even turn out to be imperative.
2. **Increases in your margins.** Can increasing your investment in personalization or customization decrease internal costs for your clients, and can you participate in the gain from those savings? Perhaps customers will be willing to pay more for the product if they know that they make up for the extra cost through process savings. Perhaps you treat the personalization as an extravalue service that makes economic sense for certain classes of customers, and you simply charge for it.

It is useful to approach your personalization investment the way you would approach most other large investments, analyzing it in terms of current and future cash flows. You can readily estimate the outgoing cash flows, both initially and year to year, of supporting a certain level of personalization. It includes the hardware, software, and services required to set up the system and the ongoing technical and marketing costs of keeping it running. Then, looking at estimated increased sales over a customer's lifetime and the effect of increased margins, you should be able to make some rough estimates about the rate of return from your investment.

You should embark on this process admitting that it is a rough estimate and that there are also important factors that are beyond estimation. For example, personalization might be a critical factor in establishing leadership in your market (a good bet in financial services, for example). The difference between market leadership and failure to lead the market is difficult to boil down into a discounted cash flow analysis. But, even given these caveats and limitations, the process is worth attempting and wrestling with. The reason is that working through the discounted cash flow analysis will help you to ask important questions and maybe even get some answers about the potential impact of different personalization approaches on your business.

We close this discussion with a simple, real-life example. In talking recently with a certain company about its focus on personalization, we found out that its estimate of the lifetime revenues from customers was around thirty dollars. Once that fact was on the table, it was clear that investing very much, per customer, on personalization was hard to justify. It turned out, in this case, that investing in building the brand made more sense than investing in personalization.

Personalization and one-to-one selling are such seductive ideas that there is a temptation to apply them everywhere. Putting the question into the analytical framework of discounted cash flows can often be a critical step in moving the discussion forward from how great personalization is, in general, to what it can do for your products and your business.

Dynamic Delivery

Thinking about costs and benefits naturally leads to looking for ways to reduce the costs while retaining the benefits. Applied to the personalization process, the question becomes "Is there some way to get most of the benefits of personalization or even customization without incurring the full cost of complete, one-on-one customization?"

Thinking about this question quickly leads to asking whether you can automatically use the same content in many different ways. Can you maintain one batch of stuff, but automatically repackage it for different customers? Can you look at a particular customer's profile, apply some fixed rules, and then automatically create customized interaction and delivery?

This is the kind of thinking that Broadvision was doing in 1993 when it offered its initial personalization and delivery platforms. It is also the thinking that has motivated other companies, such as Vignette and Art Technology Group, to enter the personalization market in the years since then. These companies offer products to deliver particular content to particular users, based on rules. Whether you buy it or whether you build it yourself, such *dynamic delivery* is an important component of your personalization system. As shown earlier in Figure 9–1 and its simple overall view of the personalization system, the dynamic delivery system typically works from the classification process in the middle of the figure out to the back end, providing high-speed, one-to-one delivery.

Dynamic versus Static

Understanding what dynamic delivery is all about is easier if we begin with a quick look at the difference between static and dynamic web pages. Knowing how pages are assembled and delivered will make it easier to understand what is involved in supporting personalized page delivery.

A *static* web page is an HTML file that sits on the server, completely assembled, waiting for someone to view it. It may be a very complex page, with a lot of animated graphics, HTML forms, and links to other pages, but it is all of a piece. With the recent advent of very capable, flexible web page layout software, designers typically create static pages with a visual design tool that allows them to see what the pages will look like as they build them. Then they save each page, knowing that, later, when a page is called up on someone's web browser, it will look very nearly the way it looked in the design tool and will contain the content that the designer put into it. It is the same page for anyone who comes to view it.

A *dynamic* page, on the other hand, is assembled on the fly, typically by pulling different pieces of the page from a large, fast storage cache that acts as a kind of specialized database of page parts. The on-the-fly assembly is driven by scripts or rules that run on the server. The scripts can automatically respond to information about the user collected in cookies and profiles. They can also randomize the content so that if a user returns to a site that contains advertising, he or she is likely to see different ads. Dynamic pages don't exist until someone comes to look at them. After they are delivered and after the visitor moves on, they are gone again.

There is a kind of middle ground between really static pages that are always the same for everyone and fully dynamic pages that are assembled out of parts on the server. The middle ground consists of static pages that contain JavaScript or some other kind of program code that runs on the client computer rather than on the server. The embedded scripts can enable the page to be responsive to the customer in limited ways. Clearly, however, code that is running on the client computer has to return to the server for information about the customer from past visits, which is stored in databases.

Up until a couple of years ago, most web pages on most sites were static. Discussions at Internet conferences talked about website "publishing," with a focus on being able to take the same content that was being used for print or for CD-ROM and to make that content available on the web. All the processing and manipulation happened on the back end, focused on creating the web page. Once it was published, the page could sit on the server, ready for delivery to visitors' browsers.

The Trend Toward Dynamic

News sites were among the first to break away from this static page model. They were motivated not by concerns about personalization, but by the much more concrete, immediate fact that news changes constantly and that different kinds of stories have different useful lifespans and therefore need to be updated at different rates. Rather than renewing a news site once a day, like a newspaper, they needed to be able to update it piecemeal and continuously. (Currently, the *LA Times* site is updated in some way every two seconds.) In order to sustain such flexible, real-time publishing, a number of leading news sites, such as the *Wall Street Journal* and CNET, began building custom-made dynamic page delivery systems. Within a short while (this was all happening in Internet time), some of this work began to find its way into commercially available systems. For example, CNET's system became the starting point for off-the-shelf dynamic delivery software offered by Vignette.

In the meantime, Broadvision's early personalization server was evolving from a tool to support community sites, matching profiles to content, into a full-fledged, rule-driven dynamic content server. On the development front, more and more sites began using scripts running on the web server to customize pages for visitors, creating internally developed dynamic sites. By 1998, a large proportion of the more active commercial sites were using server-side scripting or products such as Broadvision, Vignette's Story Server, and Art Technology Group's

Dynamo to create dynamic sites. The trend over 2000 and beyond is for larger sites to rely more and more on the off-the-shelf products rather than on internally developed or custom-made solutions.

Choosing a Delivery Mechanism

So what does all of this mean for a company that is trying to put the pieces together to support personalized delivery? Combining what we know of the requirements of personalization with trends in web commerce application software, we arrive at the following suggestions:

- Personalization requires some kind of dynamic content delivery: It requires different pages for different people and different companies.
- If your personalization program is modest and if your site is not handling thousands of visitors a day, you can meet your dynamic delivery requirements through custom development of server-based scripts that assemble the right content for each customer. This is, in almost any case, certainly the place to begin with supporting personalization.
- As website traffic increases, performance becomes more critical. Hiring good, experienced technical staff or good consultants becomes very important in addressing this; they need to be aware of the costs of starting up interpreters for each request, the cost of database accesses, and the way that the content itself is stored on disk or cached in memory.
- Although some level of experimenting with personalization is almost certainly a good idea, you should try to get some grasp of the value of personalization to your company before making large investments in the dynamic delivery required to support it. As suggested, you can estimate this value through an analysis of cash flows that places the current expenditures for personalization against the anticipated cash flows from increased sales, increased margins, and reductions in customer acquisition costs. It is important to go through this exercise even if your numbers are approximate. The value is in getting you to think carefully about whether, for your business, personalization can realistically increase sales or help maintain high margins.
- Increasingly sophisticated personalization efforts will result in increased difficulty with maintaining the personalization logic in custom-made scripts. This maintenance cost, combined with the performance requirements associated with increased traffic, should lead you to consider off-the-shelf products to support dynamic delivery. This is still a young market that is growing

and changing rapidly, and the costs of dynamic delivery software applications are still relatively high. However, armed with your analysis of future cash flows, you should have some general idea of what personalization is worth to you. The cash outlay for the dynamic delivery applications can be evaluated against the decreases in cash for new development and maintenance over time.

- As more and more of your website visitors use newer versions of browsers that can do a good job of supporting use of scripts that can run on the client rather than on the server, your technical team should consider what kinds of personalization can reasonably be handled on the client. The ability to offload some of the processing from the server to the visitor's machine can potentially improve performance without greatly increasing your costs.

In short, dynamic delivery is to personalization much as a mortgage is to a house. If the house is worth having, you need the mortgage, too. The good news is that the emergence of off-the-shelf dynamic delivery software, which will inevitably decrease in cost over time, is making the house more affordable.

Personalized Information Storage

So far, we have looked at how to engage your customers in telling you what they need and at how you can support personalized responses. We noted the requirement to identify the customer and then looked at different kinds of profiles that you can build that reflect the customer's content interests, viewing preferences, and even the customer's internal business processes. We discussed the problem of finding the right point on the continuum between personalization and full customization, and we looked at the different tools and approaches available to you to support the dynamic delivery that is implied by personalization and customization. Throughout all of this discussion, our focus has been on delivering *your* content to the customer.

It is also useful, however, to consider ways to manage the *customer's* content. If you think about the goal of personalization, which is to create a relationship with the customer that earns you the right to be a preferred supplier, it is clear that the process of storing and using the customer's information, in appropriate ways, is another way to reach toward that goal.

To take a simple example, I buy a fair amount of computer and electronics hardware over the Internet. There are a few suppliers who already have my credit card numbers and shipping information on file. In a couple of cases, these companies also maintain (and, most importantly, provide me with access to) records of what I have purchased, when I purchased it, and what I paid, along with invoice numbers. In terms of sorting out my own imperfect record keeping, it has sometimes been very handy to be able to go back to these vendors and get a report, at any time of day or night, of what I have purchased. (It always seems that I do my bookkeeping and discovery of missing records late at night.)

Like any Internet shopper, I pay attention to price, using automated tools to obtain and compare prices on computer equipment. But the interesting thing is that price is not the only factor in my purchasing. If I find that the hardware that I want is available from one of the suppliers who has all my account information on file, I will typically buy it from that supplier, even if it is available someplace else for $10 or $15 less. For that vendor, this is the kind of fact that can go into the calculation of the value of personalization. Assuming that the hardware is worth a few hundred dollars, this vendor can increase its margin by as much as 5 percent simply by establishing a relationship with me and keeping track of my information for me.

Storing the customer's information becomes a more powerful component in your business relationship with customers as you find useful ways to put that information to work for the customer. The *Wall Street Journal Interactive Edition,* once again, provides a good example. As part of the *Journal*'s Personal Edition, each subscriber can keep track of up to 30 different investments in a portfolio. The investments can be U.S. stocks, mutual funds, options, or stocks on different exchanges. The subscriber enters the number of shares held and the purchase price, and the *Journal* automatically calculates the current value and the gain on the investments, using current prices.

Business-to-business environments provide rich opportunities for putting the customer's information to work for that customer. For example, Equilinx is an Internet-based parts and services exchange for the marine repair industry. Port engineers, who are responsible for locating repair parts and making sure that they are waiting on the dock ready for installation when the ship returns to port, often have difficulty simply identifying failed components (the ship is at sea; the engineer is in port), much less finding suitable replacements (there is a good chance that the failed equipment is 15 years old and hasn't been manufactured in that form for a decade). To address this problem, Equilinx, which is still in the early phases of developing its online exchange, plans to work closely with companies that build and maintain complete inventories of all the equipment on each ship owned by a shipping company, along with cross-listings of possible replacements.

By organizing the record keeping for port engineers, Equilinx hopes to become the preferred source for obtaining bids on replacement equipment.

Business relationships translate into repeat business, lower cost of sales, and therefore higher net margins. When you progress to the point with a customer where your company is entrusted with the customer's information, which may sometimes be confidential information, you clearly have a "relationship" in this useful, productive sense. Web marketers talk about "stickiness." Stickiness is good—it means that the customer keeps coming back, rather than leaping from supplier to supplier just on the basis of price. The fact that you have the customer's information and trust and that other vendors don't is a substantial source of stickiness and advantage.

Building this kind of relationship takes time and happens in steps. Here are some suggestions:

- First, and most important, understand and focus on the customer's problem, as well as your own. Acquiring this understanding is not easy. National Semiconductor spent a great deal of time interviewing hardware design engineers to make sure that it really understood, in detail, how they approached the design process. Equilinx is staffed with port engineers and is spending a great deal of time talking with other port engineers and with shipping companies just to make sure that it understands what is currently "broken" from the customer's point of view.
- Along with thinking about the information that you can provide to the customer, do think carefully about how you can help the customers make better use of their own information. What can you store and keep track of for them that adds value to their processes?
- Expect to proceed in small steps. Before customers will trust Equilinx and its partners with keeping track of all the equipment on each of their ships, it is likely that Equilinx will first have to demonstrate that it can keep track of purchase histories and provide useful accounting reports. As a next stage, perhaps customers will let Equilinx handle standing orders for replacement equipment, with Equilinx filling the orders whenever inventory drops below certain levels and when pricing is attractive. After establishing that level of confidence from the customer, then perhaps Equilinx will be able to manage component lists for entire ships and fleets.
- As with all aspects of personalization, remember that the personalization and the record keeping are not ends in themselves. Storing information for

your customers is useful insofar as it becomes one component in the foundation of a longer-term business relationship with your customers, going beyond individual transactions. You should be able to articulate and plan that relationship as a whole. In particular, you should be able to say how growing and how maintaining the relationship are good for your business, as well as for the customer's business. Then you can fit storage of the customer's information into the plan in context.

The Self-Describing Marketplace

All of the approaches to personalization that we have looked at so far build on information volunteered by the customers. They may be setting up a profile, or they may be giving you some information to keep track of for them so that they can use it on your site (portfolio holdings, ship specifications), but, in each case, the customers are knowingly and willingly trusting you with information. There is nothing sneaky or surreptitious going on here behind the scenes. You make a calculation about the costs and benefits to you of providing personalized content and service, they make a calculation about the risks and benefits of sharing the information, and the deal is done.

There is a really nice side benefit for you in these deals: You are getting a detailed picture of your market that you would otherwise have to pay a great deal of money for, if you could get it at all. By aggregating and surveying the portfolio information provided by subscribers, the *Wall Street Journal* could focus news and features so that it better reflects the subscriber's interests (e.g., biotech stocks). Looking at the overall equipment listings for ships, Equilinx could do a better job of anticipating requirements and building relationships with suppliers.

Perhaps even more important than such direct descriptions of your customers is the fact that all of this information is raw material for market segmentation efforts. Put another way, the information about individual customers becomes a critical part of defining the customer groups that were identified earlier in Figure 9–1 as a critical part of the personalization process.

As each of you who have worked with marketing issues already knows, market segmentation is often difficult, demanding work. The utility of the segmentation scheme depends on two things:

1. Dividing customers into groups so that the members of each group behave in the same way in some important respect.

2. Knowing enough other information about the members of the group so that you can make useful connections between customer attributes ("buyers of French red wines") and behaviors that matter to you ("tend to spend more on gourmet breads").

The profile information and stored data from your customers can help you with each of these objectives. For example, using the ship inventory information in combination with other customer profile information as it builds its business over the coming months, Equilinx could get answers to questions such as, If we look at our most valuable customers—the ones in the top 10 percent in terms of our revenues from transactions—what does this group have in common? Is it the age of the ships? Or perhaps the kind of operation that they are engaged in (e.g., tankers versus bulk container)? The duty cycle of the ships (e.g., tugs that are always starting and stopping versus long-distance transport ships)? Or is it that the ships have certain kinds of systems and components that become the basis for the business?

Clearly, being able to answer such questions could be an important step toward building more high-value business. You might expect to spend a lot of money on surveys and other tools to develop the picture of your customers required to support such a segmentation effort. One of the nice things about engaging your customers in the dialogue required to support personalization is that you get the information that you need for free.

We will look much more closely at the role of groups in creating customer engagement in Chapter 10.

Privacy

It should go without saying that the process of collecting and maintaining detailed information about each of your customers implies a contract based on trust. It is to your advantage to make that contract explicit, putting your commitment to protecting the customer's information within the privacy statement on your website. It would take only a single mistake with a customer's profile information or private data to put you out of the personalization business. This is particularly true in business-to-business settings, where news travels very fast and where there is no tolerance for breach of faith. As was stressed in our earlier discussion of privacy, the most common mistakes in this area are not due to lack of policy or intent, but arise from the failure to shape the company's values around protection of the customer's information. The biggest risks tend to be from well-meaning employees who are seeking some short-term advantage for your company and who don't comprehend the larger consequences of compromising customer information. Breaches of privacy cannot just be against the rules—they need to be unthinkable.

Summary

This chapter puts in place the foundation for thinking carefully and analytically about personalization. Personalization works by combining information about individual customers with information about customer groupings. The combined inputs enable output back to the customer of information that is of particular interest to that customer. The most direct and usually least expensive source of information about individual customers is the customers themselves. You gather information about needs and preferences simply by asking for it. Getting information from customers in this way should be viewed as a kind of trade. Customers will tell you more about themselves when there is clear benefit to their doing so.

The decision to personalize your interaction with customers is not a binary one. Instead, your investment in personalization can range from relatively simple initiatives that give customers some small control over presentation style and content to full-fledged, separate extranets for different customers. Although we use the term *personalization* to cover this full range of initiatives, it is useful to recognize that your choices form a continuum ranging from simple personalization to full-fledged *customization*.

It is useful to approach the question of where your efforts should fall along this continuum through use of an evaluation framework built around discounted cash flow analysis. Although the future incoming cash flows are necessarily often rough estimates, the process of working through the analysis is important because it can help you think more clearly about which of your expectations and plans have reasonable chance of success and which reflect more enthusiasm than real possibility. The cash flow analysis provides a good tool for evaluating and thinking more carefully about your different investments in personalization and customer engagement.

Personalization implies access to some mechanism that allows you to deliver different content to different customers. Options available to you range from simple server-side scripting to fully dynamic delivery where pages are assembled on the fly. Purchasing, building, and maintaining the delivery system can be a major source of expense in building a personalization system. Most companies find that they can approach development of dynamic delivery capabilities in stages.

In addition to thinking of personalization in terms of information that you deliver to customers, it is also useful to think in terms of information that you can store and manage for these customers. Managing information for these customers is a great way to tie the customer more closely to your business.

Handling customer information is also a way to learn more about your customers, creating a self-describing marketplace. Aggregating and analyzing information across your customers should enable you to divide customers into useful segments and groups. For reasons that we will explore in more detail in Chapter 10, creating customer groupings is an important part of being able to anticipate and serve customer needs.

Naturally, the process of collecting and managing information about customers works only if customers can trust you to take good care of that information by respecting privacy and confidentiality. The kinds of personalization activity described in this chapter—engaging the customer—must build on your attention to being a trustworthy partner.

Key Ideas

- Personalization is driven from information that the customer provides for you. It is useful to think of this as an explicit, open exchange, where customers understand the benefit that they are getting in return for the information that they are providing.
- Building customer relationships is good business. As such, the investment in customer engagement should be evaluated like any other investment. Although the process certainly involves some guesswork, use of discounted cash flow analysis as part of your evaluation framework is a good way to focus on personalization investments that will yield real net benefit.
- Dynamic delivery is a necessary part of personalized delivery. You have a range of options open to you here, and you can usually grow into a more sophisticated approach to delivery as you come to better understand what kinds of personalization are most effective.
- The process of storing and managing information for your customers is both a good way to learn more about them and a good way to build tighter engagement.

CHAPTER TEN

Customers as Members of Groups

Objectives of This Chapter

- Show why understanding how your customers fit into larger groups is important.
- Provide a "big picture" view of how to develop and use information about groupings of customers.
- Describe the operation and use of recommendation engines.
- Describe approaches to defining customer segments.
- Help you understand how to usefully combine recommendation engines, segmentation, and other approaches to working with your customers as members of groups.

Focusing on the Group

In Chapter 9 we looked carefully at all the different kinds of things that you can learn about your customers simply by asking them. We saw that if you can provide real value to customers in response to the information that they provide, you can set up relationships where you keep track not only of their viewing and content preferences but also of inventory data, product specifications, and other information about their business that allows you to serve them better. Connecting more closely to your customer in this way results in a relationship that is more profitable for both you and the customer.

At the beginning of Chapter 9, however, we said that data about each individual customer is only one of the inputs to the personalization process. The other input is information about the *groups* of customers that you serve. We illustrated the relationships of these inputs to the overall process in a simple diagram of the personalization process (Figure 9–1). We reproduce that diagram here, in Figure 10–1, extending it to include new features related to understanding the makeup and interests of customer groups, which are the focus of this chapter.

There are two reasons that working with groups, in addition to working with individual customers, is important:

1. **It simplifies personalization.** Dealing with every customer in a completely unique way is very expensive. As noted in Chapter 9 in our discussions of personalization and customization and cost-benefit analysis, there certainly are times when the benefits of providing a fully customized site for a customer

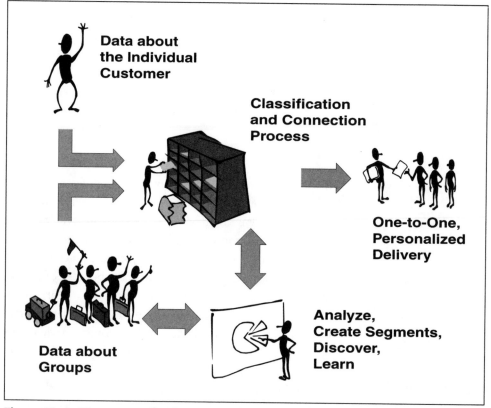

Figure 10–1 The personalization process, expanded to focus on groups

justify the costs, but this is typically not the case for all your customers. In order to provide less expensive kinds of personalization, you need to be able to create "baskets" of content and services that are uniform for a particular group of customers. Then personalization can consist of providing an individual with prepackaged content from each of the baskets in which he or she has interest. Put another way, you simplify the personalization process by reducing it from responding to every customer in a unique way to preparing responses for a number of predefined groups. The customer's uniqueness is expressed through the combination of groups in which he or she is a member.

2. **You can often sell more to the individual if you understand the needs of the group.** Anticipating what customers need next and what else they need that they aren't yet asking for is much simpler when you understand something about the groups to which each customer belongs. As an example, Wine.com (www.wine.com, formerly "Virtual Vineyards"), a site selling wine over the Internet, saw that Italian wines were not selling as well as the company felt that they should. It decided to create a personalized, targeted promotion for customers who were likely to buy Italian wines but who weren't already buying them. As many of you know, selling something new to an existing customer is referred to as "cross-selling." The hard question that Wine.com had to answer, of course, was which customers were likely buyers for the cross-sell. This isn't just a question about individuals; it is also a question about groups. The way to approach the problem is to first divide customers into groups that represent different kinds of buyers. Next, you identify the customers that, as a group, tend to buy a lot of Italian wine. Then you look inside these groups to find the individual members who are not yet buying much Italian wine. If you do a good job of creating groups of buyers with similar tastes, there is an excellent chance that these individuals are good prospects for additional Italian wine sales. It turns out that Personify (see end-of-chapter reference 1), the company that supplied the software to Wine.com to perform this analysis, found out that some groups were four times as likely to respond to an Italian wine promotion as others. The point is that information about groups is important to predicting the needs and preferences of individuals.

In short, you need information about groups, in addition to information about individuals, so that you can make the personalization process cost-effective and so that you can make predictions about additional customer needs. These predictions can be incorporated into the personalized interaction between your company and your customer to expand sales.

How do you build a picture of customer groups? You don't interact directly with groups; you interact with customers. Consequently, there must be some way to pull the individual customer profiles and customer actions together into a bigger picture. We will explore three different approaches to creating and characterizing groups:

1. Recommendation engines
2. Software-assisted segmentation that works on your data from log files and customer profiles
3. Informed judgment by the marketer

In practice, companies often use a combination of these three approaches. When we consider the little marketing person in the lower part of Figure 10–1 as he or she analyzes, creates segments, discovers, and learns, we can safely assume that a combination of tools and resources is being used. But let's start out by examining them as distinct options before we look at how to blur them together.

Recommendation Engines

A *recommendation engine* provides an automatic way to associate an individual customer with a larger group so that you can make purchase recommendations to the individual. With a recommendation engine, you can say to the customer, "Here are some of the things that other people with interests like yours are buying; you might find that you will like them, too."

Regular shoppers on the CDnow site (www.cdnow.com), for example, have the option of asking CDnow to make suggestions about other recordings that they might like. Working from information about their past purchases, augmented by their reactions to some recommended recordings, CDnow comes up with a list of CDs. The site provides the customers with sample tracks so that they can try before they buy. We note incidentally that, according to recent research by Jupiter Communications (see end-of-chapter reference 2), CDnow receives 59 percent of its revenues from repeat sales. Considered in terms of the lifetime customer value and cost-benefit analysis introduced in Chapter 9, CDnow is clearly a good candidate for using recommendation engines and other forms of personalization. Arguably, the high customer return rate is also a consequence of the fact that the company is already doing so.

For a firsthand taste of what recommendation engines do, you can go to a site called the "Movie Critic" (www.moviecritic.com). The Movie Critic recommends movies based on your ratings of movies that you have seen in the past. If you have never experienced what recommendation engines can do, the Movie Critic is an easy site to experiment with since it doesn't involve your needing to buy anything in order to provide a list of your preferences. It is interesting and instructive to watch how, as you rate more movies, the recommendations quickly become more accurate.

Like so much else about the technologies associated with your web business, it is helpful to have a general idea of *how* recommendation engines work before you start thinking about *whether* they will work for you and your business. Knowing something about what goes on inside them is the easiest way to know what they do well and where they can add value.

How They Work

Most recommendation engines use an approach known as *collaborative filtering*. The name is an apt description of the process. It works by filtering recommendations through the preferences of collaborators who share your tastes and interests.

Imagine that we knew the library classification numbers for the last three books that you have read. This would allow us to create a three-dimensional graph, with library classification numbers on each axis, and to fix a point in the graphing space that identified your recent reading choices.

It would be a pretty safe bet that other people whose points were close to yours shared similar reading interests. If we knew the titles of the books that they read, it might be worthwhile to recommend those titles to you.

This is a very simplified example of what recommendation engines do. They calculate a "position" in a multidimensional space (many more than three dimensions) that represents your preferences and interests. Rather than just working with identical dimensions, as in our example where each axis was a library classification number, commercial recommendation engines cope with different kinds of measures (e.g., preference ratings, profile data, purchase history, links that the customer has clicked on) scaled in different ways. They locate the individual customer in the space formed by these complex measures and then identify the other customers with similar interests and preferences. These other customers become the reference group used to provide new recommendations for the individual.

Performance and Forming Groups

The idea behind a recommendation engine is pretty simple: Find people with similar preferences and then use the aggregate purchase patterns as recommendations for the individual group members. But this can be a notoriously difficult idea to implement when there are many measures, many customers, new customers coming into the system making new purchases, established customers changing their positions as they make additional purchases, and so on. The graph is in constant motion, and the relationships are complex, making the computation of the relative strength of relationships very difficult. To make things worse, the system has to operate in real time, making recommendations on the fly as the user needs them.

The key to solving this problem in a commercial system is in recognizing that group profiles naturally shift more slowly than individual profiles. If I buy a CD recommended to me because my group is all listening to it, that act changes information about me but doesn't impact the group. The problem is more complicated than that, of course, because most individuals belong to several groups. Even so, the fact that group preferences represent an average of many individual preferences means that group profiles change more slowly. This opens up the possibility of confining real-time calculations to examining the relation of the individual to the groups rather than to always redefining the groups. In practice, different vendors approach this differently (see the Technical Note), but all vendors find some way of freezing the definitions of the reference groups in order to make the problem solvable.

What this means is that you can think of a recommendation engine as an automatic way to break your customer population into groups. It may be that you are not able to "look inside" the process so that you can see and name the

---

Technical Note: Reducing the Computational Complexity

As noted in the text, there are different ways to solve the problem of reducing the computational complexity within recommendation engines. All approaches depend on reducing the number of separate profiles that need to be recalculated as the individual buyer makes a purchase or in some other way indicates new preferences. The goal is to have the system immediately reflect the new preference information from the individual and to produce new, accurate recommendations that take that information into account while at the same time not having to recalculate everything else. (Remember, there are many buyers who are active at once, effectively changing the reference points for every other buyer.)

There are basically two approaches to simplifying this problem enough to make it practically solvable:

1. Reduce the complexity of the calculation by aggregating the individuals into groups of people with strongly similar tastes and interests. The average, or typical, preferences of the group are used in place of all the individual preferences. This approach greatly reduces the number of points in the graph. Moreover, since the groups tend to change more slowly than individuals, this approach takes the edge off the recalculation problem as individuals in the groups continue to make new purchases. Recommendations are with reference to the group or groups to which an individual belongs rather than with reference to the individual per se. The theoretical advantage of this approach is that groups can be used as the basis for market segmentation (which we will discuss in more detail later).

2. Continue to work with individuals and with individual preferences, but simplify the problem by looking at them in relation to a set of "mentors" (individuals with similar preferences) rather than in relation to the whole population. Essentially, this approach addresses the problem by breaking it into two stages. First, find good mentors (this can be done in background processing rather than in real time). Then perform the individual preference calculations against only this smaller (and temporarily frozen) set of mentor profiles. The theoretical advantage of this approach is that it might permit finer-grained judgments since every individual could have a different set of mentors (i.e., there is a separate, unique reference group for each individual).

The recommendation engine from NetPerceptions (see end-of-chapter reference 3) uses an approach that is closer to the first method. A product known as "LikeMinds," offered by Andromedia (see end-of-chapter reference 4) now owned by Macromedia, uses the second method. Each vendor, of course, claims that its approach produces the most accurate recommendations.

groups in the same way that you would if you formed the groups as part of a conscious marketing segmentation effort, but they are there. This will be a valuable, useful insight as you work to integrate your investments in recommendation engines, segmentation work, and other marketing research intended to help you better understand your customers.

Integration with Different Information Sources

One of the most attractive features of recommendation engines is that they can automatically extract value from the many different data sources available to you on your website. You have information about particular pages that a customer visits and about the links that he or she clicks on. You certainly know what a customer buys. You have profile information provided by the customer in setting up the site to reflect individual needs and preferences, and you can ask the customer directly about preferences, just as the Movie Critic does. Recommendation engines can integrate all of these information sources in their effort to create suggestions about additional purchases. Each source contributes new dimensions to preference space used to define, separate, and group your different customers.

It may be obvious, but it is important to note that such integration of disparate data is not a "plug-and-go" operation but rather something that will require careful thought and design investment. As a simple example of the kind of subtlety that one can encounter here, suppose you were setting up a recommendation system that, like the CDnow site, makes recommendations on the basis of recordings that you own and that you are purchasing. Assume that you have an entry for a customer who bought a lot of Beatles albums between 1965 and 1967 and a lot of Nirvana in 1991 and 1992. You have a second customer who just bought Beatles and Nirvana albums this year. Are new purchases today by the first buyer good recommendations for the second buyer? Probably not. The first buyer bought new music as it came out; the second buyer is following much later in the market. Clearly, the time of purchase might matter as much as what was purchased. As we said, setting up a recommendation engine is not just a plug-and-go deal but requires some careful thought about your customers, informed by information from outside the recommendation engine.

Integration with Marketer Input

Most commercial recommendation engines include ways to reflect information that your marketing staff has about the market in addition to information collected directly by the engine. The most obvious example of the need for such other inputs is when you have a new product that you would like to recommend. Let's say that you are selling books, and a new John Grisham novel comes out. You want to promote it, but to whom do you recommend it? No one has purchased it yet, so the recommendation engine isn't going to automatically recommend it on the basis of historical group profiles. How do you seed the system?

Commercial recommendation engines give you a way to solve problems like this with hand-built rules. You probably want to recommend the book to people who have read other John Grisham books. You also know that people who read John Grisham also tend to buy novels by Scott Turow, so you want to recommend the new Grisham book to Turow readers. (How do you know? We'll talk about this later.) The general approach used in most products is to let you set up imaginary customers who have bought the new Grisham book. The system folds these customers into the group profiles and begins to recommend the new book. As people actually start buying it, the recommendations become more sophisticated and precise.

Reasons to Use a Recommendation Engine

Now that we know what they do and something about how they do it, we can begin to think carefully about the situations in which a recommendation engine will provide the most benefit to a web business. Here is a list of the advantages that recommendation engines provide:

- They are automatic. Once they are set up, they keep making recommendations, typically making them with more and more precision as the amount of information that they operate on grows. A related point: The updating of their information and recommendations happens automatically.
- They integrate a great deal of complicated information to make connections and recommendations that would be difficult for a human marketer. In other words, they can come up with good cross-sells that would never otherwise occur to you.
- Classification and grouping of customers can be based directly on preference—the thing that you are most interested in when making a recommendation—rather than on secondary information such as age, income, and so on.
- They operate without any setup or explicit profile information from the buyer, working instead from implicit preference information indicated through purchases and website behavior.

- They deliver personalized recommendations to a wide variety of customers. The recommendations are not "one size fits all" but grow directly from the individual customer profile.

When Recommendation Engines Aren't Useful

For all of their strengths, recommendation engines are not a good fit for all web businesses. Consider, for example, the cross-selling that needs to be done by Equilinx, the company that we looked at earlier that is selling repair and replacement parts and systems for ships. Given the focused mission of the customers, it is clearly absurd to be telling someone who is buying a replacement pump that other customers buying pumps have also been buying replacement generators.

This does not mean that there aren't opportunities for cross-selling and up-selling at Equilinx. In fact, it will often be the case that customers will be interested in up-sells in the form of new components with better performance or lower operating costs that can be substituted for older components. They will also be interested in cross-sells that recommend replacing associated systems; when replacing a generator, they might also consider replacing the regulator and control systems. The fact that cross-selling and up-selling is important here but is not enhanced through the use of recommendation engines raises some interesting questions: Why don't recommendation engines work here? What is different about Equilinx?

Since cross-selling depends on connecting an individual to the broader buying patterns of a group, it is tempting to suggest that perhaps groups don't matter as much on a site like Equilinx. Perhaps the only thing that matters at such narrow, goal-oriented sites, as opposed to sites like CDnow, is the individual buyer and his or her immediate objectives. (The customer is looking for a particular replacement bearing or winch rather than for interesting music.)

Closer examination of the Equilinx customer base argues strongly against such a hypothesis. The marine industry is highly segmented, as even a quick look at the trade magazines serving the industry demonstrates. There are groups interested just in tugboats, others in the tanker business, others who focus on container ships, and yet others who specialize in the marine operations to support offshore oil drilling. Each of these groups has very distinct needs and interests and represents a genuinely different customer segment and a different set of market opportunities for Equilinx. Understanding the needs of groups and serving those needs certainly do matter.

What is different about Equilinx, then, that makes recommendation engines less useful here than on other sites? Here are some important factors:

- **The buying groups on the Equilinx site are already well defined.** Recommendation engines are most useful when the boundaries between groups are fuzzy and flexible. People buying CDs, books, or other consumer goods certainly do fit into interest groups, but there is usually crossover. A customer might enjoy both Bach and techno. There is much less likelihood of crossover between someone servicing brown-water tugs and a port engineer maintaining container ships. The effect of the sharper, cleaner boundaries is that the magic of recommendation engines, which is their ability to see connections that are too complex for most human analysts, is less valuable.

- **Cross-selling and up-selling are not primarily a matter of preference.** When a pump fails, finding a replacement is not a matter of understanding my preferences about pumps. The purchase needs to meet specific requirements regarding flow rates, size of fittings, and so on. In such cases the cross-selling and up-selling are best left to a human with subject matter expertise rather than to a machine working on statistical relationships. Knowing that a particular new pump design is an excellent upgrade and replacement for an older model is the kind of thing that an engineer does very well. Software is not a good or necessary replacement.

- **Combinations of items in a purchase are not necessarily generalizable.** The foundation upon which recommendation engines work depends on an assumption. The assumption is that the particular combination of items purchased by one buyer is relevant to predicting the needs and preferences of other buyers in the same group. The fact that someone buys a John Grisham novel and then a Scott Turow novel is, in fact, relevant in making a recommendation to other John Grisham readers. But the fact that I have a fishing boat that needs a generator overhaul and a replacement ice machine has no relevance at all to someone else who just has a failing generator, even if he or she is a fishing boat operator. The combination of purchases is strictly need based rather than preference based.

These business factors suggest a set of questions that you might ask about your business as you consider the use of recommendation engines: Is the primary focus of the purchases based on clearly defined needs? Is the selection of the items making up an order a matter of preference, or is it primarily due to external factors (as in the generator and ice machine example)? Is preference a significant factor in selecting a particular model of a product (e.g., which model of a Palm Pilot is best for you?), or is the selection primarily a technical evaluation of cost, form, fit, and function? Is the segmentation of your market relatively straight-forward, which is to say that a human marketer could accurately define the segments, or are there complex subgroups splitting off and combining preferences from larger groups, which is the kind of situation where software can really help?

These questions are not the same as hard-and-fast rules. It may turn out, in fact, that Equilinx could find innovative, important applications for a recommendation engine that we are not seeing here. Perhaps, for certain products, the preferences and experiences of others could usefully be captured in the operation of a recommendation engine. Our intent is simply to help you think in more careful, precise ways about just where recommendation engines will do you the most good, tying the principles underlying their operation in a useful way to your business needs.

Selecting the Right Product

A number of vendors offer recommendation engines. We list some of them in the references at the end of this chapter. If you decide that you need a recommendation engine, you will probably talk to these companies, along with others. What should you be looking for? Here are some general suggestions:

- **Accuracy.** Making inappropriate recommendations to your customers is worse than not recommending anything at all. For example, one of the major book and music shopping sites was recently using a recommendation engine to tell book buyers what CDs were being bought by people who had the same reading interests. As someone who buys a lot of technology books, the music recommendations were, at best, entertaining. They certainly showed that the range of musical tastes among people involved in technology is, in a word, "broad." This is an extreme example, but it illustrates the point that customers will reach a conclusion very quickly about whether your automated recommendations are worth bothering with or whether they are a nuisance.
- **Flexibility.** Competing products provide varying capabilities for working with the different kinds of customer information that you have on your site. You should begin with an inventory of the sources of information that you expect to use. They can include, among other things, explicit preference

information in response to questionnaires, "click stream" data coming from a customer's current actions, information from log files about a customer's past actions on a site, purchase information coupled with time of purchase, external demographic profile information, and information about cross-sells and up-sells that come from your own marketing information. The vendor should be able to explain in detail how the product takes advantage of these sources.

- **Performance scaled to your needs.** Recommendation engines need to work in real time. Most products perform well even on sites with large numbers of customers and purchases. The vendor should be able to describe the conditions under which performance might degrade. Where are the limits?
- **Access to group profiles.** We have explained that recommendation engines work by creating some kind of implicit grouping of your customers. Competing products differ in how they do this. One consequence of the differences in approach is that some products can provide you with a picture of how they are dividing up your customer population and others cannot or can do it only with difficulty. The value of such a picture is that your marketing organization can make important use of such understanding of the customer population. We will explore such use in the next section.

The accuracy criterion is probably both the most important factor and the most difficult one to evaluate. Because the internal mechanisms used in competing products differ, it is very likely that their ability to make accurate predictions will differ, particularly on customer populations that have specialized needs and interests. It would be very difficult—perhaps impossible—to make an evaluation for a particular population strictly on a theoretical evaluation of the different technical approaches. You really need to try the systems, on your data, with your customers. This is particularly important for business-to-business applications working with customer populations that are much different from the more general population coming to a big consumer site.

Tools for Marketing

Although recommending other products to buyers is important, it is only a part of the overall marketing effort needed to increase purchasing by existing customers and to reach new customers. You need to understand how to bring customers to your site in the first place, which means knowing where to find potential buyers whose needs and interests are most like the buyers who are already active on your site. You need to be able to evaluate different advertising and promotional efforts with regard to their ability to bring in such buyers. You need to understand how the different groups of customers contribute to the business and whether there are trends that will cause those contributions to change over time. In short, you need to be able to *think* about your customers.

Recommendation engines are designed to automate the process of creating cross-sell and up-sell opportunities. The very fact of the automation means that the recommendation engine isn't necessarily giving you and your marketing organization anything to help with your thinking. It provides great information to your customers and much less information to you.

Wine.com's experience with finding the right advertising mix is a good example of what we mean when we talk about "thinking" about customers and illustrates the kind of information that you need to do such thinking. We talked about Wine.com earlier in this chapter when we used this company's campaign to increase sales of Italian wines as an example of cross-selling.

Wine.com recognized that, for its business, like so many others, there was some kind of 80/20 rule going on when it came to customers. In fact, when the company worked through several months' worth of log file data and transaction histories, it found that there was a group of core visitors that accounted for about 80 percent of the company's revenues. Core visitors were about ten times as likely to make a purchase as the average visitor. Naturally, Wine.com wanted to know, "How do we find more of them?"

The general answer, of course, was through advertising and promotion. At the time, most of Wine.com's advertising was being done on the web. The problem for Wine.com, as for any company, was figuring out how to make the advertising expenditures as effective as possible. Before working to identify the characteristics of the core visitor population, Wine.com measured effectiveness by looking at "click through" rates: Which advertising sites produced the highest number of visitors clicking through to the Wine.com site for each dollar spent?

The ability to identify a core visitor segment and to articulate the general characteristics of the people who made up that segment provided an alternative approach to measuring effectiveness. The question could become "Which advertisements bring us the greatest number of prospective core visitors per dollar spent?" Looking at the problem in this way changed Wine.com's view of what was really working. It turned out that the site that had been regarded as the leading advertising venue was actually producing very few prospective core visitors and that other sites were quite effective at bringing in the desired visitors. By focusing on core visitors rather than on visitors in general, Wine.com was able to effect a 75 percent reduction in spending on web advertising while increasing the number of new prospective core visitors.

If we take the Wine.com experience apart and analyze it, three critical factors emerge:

1. Wine.com was able to work through log file and transaction histories to identify a clearly defined core group of buyers.
2. The company's marketing team was able to characterize that group in ways other than their buying.
3. They were able to use the group characterization to recognize new prospective members of the group.

As anyone who has spent much time thinking about marketing knows, Wine.com was using the data from its website to *segment* its customer base and market. In a web business, where it is relatively inexpensive to collect data about individual customers, it is useful to distinguish carefully between *customer base* and *market*. If possible, you want to approach segmentation from two directions, working both from your customers out to the market and from the market into your customers. Each direction requires different tools and produces a different view of your customers.

Market Segments

It is useful to be able to place the customers that you serve within the larger context of the market and the population as a whole. If you are selling to consumers, what are they like? Are they young? Female? How much do they earn? If you can answer questions like these, it becomes much easier to find more potential customers like the ones that you are already serving. The same style of question can be applied to business customers. What size companies do you serve? Are they grouped geographically? What businesses are they in?

An excellent example of how this kind of segmentation can work is SRI's "VALS" survey and segmentation scheme (see end-of-chapter reference 5). The site includes an online survey that you can take to find out which consumer segment best describes your needs and interests.

VALS is a *psychographic* segmentation scheme in that it attempts to classify consumers by motivation: Are they driven primarily by principle, status, or action? On a second axis, it classifies consumers on the basis of financial resources.

For example, someone with lesser resources who is motivated by principle is a "Believer." With greater resources this same person would be classified as "Fulfilled." Someone with lesser resources who is motivated by status is a "Striver." With more money to spend, the person would be an "Achiever."

The great value in establishing such groupings is that, over time, by surveying a great many consumers, it is possible to make fairly detailed predictions about the interests and activities of people in these groups. For example, a "Fulfilled" person is likely to have an in-ground swimming pool, use spreadsheet software, stay in ski resorts, and own a station wagon. People in this group tend not to watch drag racing on TV or to drink malt liquor. An "Achiever" is also likely to have a swimming pool, as well as a snowblower and outdoor lighting fixtures. His or her taste in cars tends more to those with sunroofs. He or she typically does not attend classical music concerts.

The value of this information to a marketer is that if you know into which segment a consumer falls, you can make decisions about what kinds of items or product features are most likely to provide cross-sell and up-sell opportunities. The VALS data also includes information that can be applied directly to advertising decisions. For example, if you want to reach "Believers," advertisements in *Organic Gardening, Weight Watchers Magazine, The National Examiner,* and *Prevention* are a good bet.

How do you identify the appropriate segments for consumers without having each of them fill out the VALS survey? You look at what they buy and what they read. If someone has gone to websites to purchase spreadsheet software and a ski vacation package and is also a frequent visitor to the Audubon site, it is a good bet that you are dealing with a "Fulfilled" person. If you can tie a consumer's web activities to offline information about magazine subscriptions and other activities, you can increase the probability of associating that consumer with the right segment. Back in Chapter 6 on cookies, we showed you how a company delivering targeted advertising across multiple sites could build this kind of profile, which would then allow the company to do a better job of putting the right ad in front of the right prospective buyer.

Customer Segments

The kind of psychographic and demographic profile information available through use of segmentation schemes such as VALS is a useful way to understand how your customers fit into the broader market. It is not useful, however, for answering the kinds of questions that Wine.com raised when it was trying to identify its core visitors. Such questions relate to activities on your site and in relation to your business rather than to the broader market. Answering such questions requires that you have a way to look at your customers as a market population in itself and then to find the segments that constitute your unique population. Rather than looking out, you are looking in.

Building an internal segmentation scheme that is unique to your company and to your customers starts from the same kind of information that you would use to drive a recommendation engine—preferences expressed in profiles, log file data, and information about purchases.

To get a sense of how the process of defining market segments works, let's go back to our earlier example of the three-dimensional graph built from the classifications of books that you have read recently. In our discussion of recommendation engines, we noted that your recent reading would be represented by a point on this graph and that people whose reading tastes are similar to yours would have points that were located close to yours.

If you collected and graphed the reading preference data for a great many people and then looked at the overall distribution of points, you would find that they would not be evenly distributed across the graph. Instead, there would be clusters of points that represent different groups of people with similar interests.

In our example, where the space is just three-dimensional, the clusters would look like little clouds of points floating in the space of the graph. Some of the clouds would be cigar shaped, some would be flattened in one dimension, and others might be more tightly clustered like a ball.

To the extent that the clouds were clearly separated, they would represent different segments within the population of readers. You could even name the segments, noting that some were grouped around mysteries, others around books on information science, and so on. But what do the groups "mean" for your business? What are the key "dimensions" that constitute the interests of your customers?

Dimensions is the key word here. We need to move away from the axes of the original graph, which just represented each of the three books, to a new set of axes that tell us something about the qualities of the readers. To do that, we rotate and twist the axes so that they do a better job of running lengthwise through some of the bigger clouds. This allows us to begin to assign names to the axes themselves rather than just to the clouds. In other words, we can assign meaning to the dimensions.

We might find, for example, that one axis runs through a number of clouds, separating fiction readers from nonfiction readers. Another rotation of the axes might send one through clouds of points in a way that expresses the tendency to read history books. We might even begin to change the angles between the axes so that they are no longer perpendicular (orthogonal) to each other, bending them at new angles to better fit the clouds. Axes that aren't perpendicular to each other measure dimensions that are not completely independent of each other—a situation that is likely to be true, in fact. Once we leave orthogonal, Cartesian space behind, we might as well also decide that the restriction to three dimensions is arbitrary. If we need a fourth or fifth axis to run through big clouds of points, so be it. All that means is that we have found that it takes four or five characteristics (dimensions) to characterize our customers.

What is presented here is a kind of physical, visual description of a process that identifies customer segments and the important dimensions that describe and differentiate them. In practice, the analysis and rotating and bending are performed through computations rather than visually. Much of the computation can be automatic, geared to finding axes that provide a mathematically calculable "best fit" to the clusters of points.

Wine.com went through just such a set of computations to identify the characteristics of its core visitors. It used a product from Personify (www.personify.com), a company that provides marketers with a way to try out different kinds of customer dimensions without having to get involved with the math.

One reason for going into detail with our reading preferences example is to take away some of the mystery behind market segmentation, thus giving you a feel for what the process does. You should also be able to see how segmentation is different from, yet related to, the process that is going on in a recommendation engine. Both look at the positions of different customers in a preference space. The recommendation engine uses the space to find customers that are like one another so that it can recommend a product or service. The segmentation tool, on the other hand, works to get an overall view of the customer groupings in the space and to identify the key dimensions that best describe and separate those groups.

Here are some key points to keep in mind with regard to customer segmentation products:

- Such products are available, and more will appear.
- They work on the customer data that you have collected for other personalization activities.
- Segmenting your customers helps you extract the meaning and insight that are buried in all the preference and activity data that you have collected.

- Customer segmentation can be coupled with market segmentation and recommendation: The capabilities are complementary.

This last point needs more explanation. It is what we turn our attention to next.

Applying Recommendation and Segmentation

In this chapter, we have looked at how to provide customers with better personalized service by working with them as members of groups. We have explored three different ways of putting such grouping information to use:

1. **Recommendation engines.** You make personalized recommendations on the basis of purchasing by other members of the group.
2. **Market segmentation.** You tie your customers to broader market profiles so that you can understand their needs and preferences in a context that reaches beyond your own company and its products.
3. **Customer segmentation.** You divide your customers into meaningful subgroups, or segments, so that you can focus your energies on growing the groups that are most productive for your business and can use group characteristics to provide more personalized service.

When we consider all three approaches at once, it is clear that they differ in terms of the amount of effort required by the marketing team and in the amount of information that they provide to the team. Going back to Figure 10–1 to the little marketing person who is looking at the pie charts and trying to understand the market and make decisions, note that some of the approaches engage him or her completely, and others don't involve him or her much at all. Recommendation engines operate automatically, for the most part, providing very little insight for the marketer and requiring very little active engagement. Customer segmentation work is at the other extreme, requiring active engagement and yielding potentially significant insights (which then have to be put to use). Market segmentation falls in the middle. When it is used in applications such as ad selection, market segmentation is set up to operate automatically once the segmentation model is in place. On the other hand, when it is used to answer questions such as, Should we advertise in *The New Yorker* or in *Spin?*, there is a lot of marketer engagement with the market segment information.

Because these different applications of customer grouping accomplish different things, they can often be used in combination with one another. On the other hand, as we noted in our discussion of recommendation engines, not all approaches are applicable to all web businesses. When does each approach make sense, and how can you combine them most effectively?

There is no complete or absolute answer to this question. But it certainly is possible to look at some examples and extract a few general guidelines. Table 10–1 lists a number of different web business scenarios and suggests the likely applicability of the different approaches to customer grouping. The scenarios are arranged in terms of the complexity of the market being served, with the most complex scenarios coming first. The different approaches to using customer groupings are ordered from left to right in terms of the amount of active engagement they require of the marketer.

For the first application scenario, a general consumer product site, consider sites like amazon.com that sell a wide variety of products to a wide variety of buyers. In such a business, recommendation engines can potentially add value by automating cross-selling. Market segmentation to look at customers in relation to the broader market can be very useful for driving rule-based cross-selling and up-selling (e.g., "This customer is a member of a demographic group that typically is interested in high-quality photography equipment, so let's tell him or her about the special on Nikon cameras"). It is also useful for directing advertising

Table 10–1 Recommendation and Segmentation Approaches for Different Kinds of Sites

Market Complexity	Marketer Involvement		
Scenario	Recommendation Engines	Market Segmentation	Customer Segmentation
General consumer product site	X	X	X
B2B site, broad groups of buyers	?	X	X
B2B site, well-defined buying groups, narrow technical cross-sell		?	X
Single product site		?	X

expenditures. And, finally, breaking apart the customers into segments makes a lot of sense, just as it did for Wine.com. So all three approaches to using customer grouping information are potentially applicable.

The second scenario is a business-to-business (B2B) site serving broad groups of customers. A good example of such a site is Grainger (www. grainger.com), which sells repair parts and industrial supplies. Because the buying is often constrained by specifications (e.g., a 1/2-horsepower, split-phase motor that runs at 3,600 rpm with a 1/2" shaft), there is less opportunity to make use of recommendation engines for cross-selling and up-selling than on a consumer site. There certainly are cross-sell and up-sell opportunities (e.g., perhaps you are running a special on a somewhat more expensive motor that meets the specifications and that offers higher efficiency), but preference and groupings are typically less important in setting up such offers. A simple rule will suffice.

Although VALS-style consumer market demographics and psychographics are not relevant to understanding customer groupings for this second kind of business, it probably is useful to connect customers to the broader market in other ways. For example, looking at a buyer in terms of company size and vertical market very probably will provide insight into a particular buyer's needs and buying patterns. These insights can be put to use in a personalization program for that customer. Finally, understanding the breakdown and lifetime value of different segments within the customer base is just as valuable here as it is for consumer sites.

Our next scenario is for a site like the Equilinx marine equipment site that we have already explored as an example. As we noted earlier, it is not likely that recommendation engines can contribute much to such a business. Further, because the external market is narrower than it is for a site like Grainger, there is probably relatively less insight to be gained from generalizing about external market groups. On a site like this, you can really get to know your individual buyers, and understanding the broader market boils down to understanding the needs of the vertical segments that your buyers represent. But looking inside this customer population and seeing which buyers contribute the most to revenue growth and to margins can make a great deal of sense.

The last scenario is for a single product site. Such sites are somewhat more unusual than the other categories that we have explored. It is, however, useful and interesting to think about how segmentation and groupings fit into such a business, if only to see which customer grouping models apply at this end of the spectrum of possible business models. As a concrete example, think of a software company that offers a single product for sale and downloading on the web. Clearly, cross-selling and up-selling are not an issue in such a business, so recommendation engines are out of the picture. The broader market, as potentially reflected in market segmentation, is, of course, important since it is where new customers come from. But the broader market questions are almost certainly simpler than they are for companies offering a more complex product line. The key questions would have to do with understanding more about the general characteristics of the current customers. For instance, in making advertising decisions, it would be useful to know which magazines were favored by the most productive buying group. All of this means, of course, that looking in some detail at the segmentation within the customer population is potentially a very productive focus. You want to be able to recognize potential customers when they come to the site.

As we look back over these cases, some generalizations emerge:

- As the buying becomes more focused and goal oriented, driven by external factors (e.g., the horsepower of the motor that needs to be replaced) rather than by preference, recommendation engines become less useful.
- As the markets become narrower and more well defined, the value of sophisticated market segmentation decreases—it reduces to knowing the vertical market and the company size for each customer. This is clearly very important information and can be used with great effect in personalization, but you don't need sophisticated market segment schemes or databases to identify the appropriate segment.
- In all cases, knowing more about your customers, especially being able to identify the characteristics of your most valuable customers, is a good thing. Consequently, customer segmentation work of some kind, even if it is just a simple manual attempt to characterize key buying groups, is almost always worth doing.

Summary

We have covered a number of difficult, important topics in this chapter. Many businesspeople, even ones closely connected to marketing operations in a web business, get recommendation engines, personalization, and different kinds of segmentation all tied together and confused. One of the primary goals of the chapter has been to help you untangle these different approaches to understanding your customers as members of groups.

Creating groupings of customers, or *segmenting* them, is important for a number of reasons. One is that personalization becomes more manageable if you can aggregate your responses to customer needs into groups. Rather than having truly unique responses for each individual, you have personalized responses that reflect group memberships. Another reason that grouping is important is that the buying activities of the group can be used to drive cross-selling and up-selling to the members of the group. Yet another reason is that grouping your customers can help you connect them to matters outside your company, such as the magazines that are read by members of a particular vertical market group. Finally, the process of creating and understanding customer groupings is critical to making the business more efficient and productive. Who are your most valuable customers, and how do you find more of them?

We explored three different approaches to working with customer groups. Each approach is associated with a different technology or methodology.

The first approach uses *recommendation engines* to suggest other purchases or options to a customer. The recommendation engine operates by connecting a customer to other customers with similar preferences. Connections can be based on a variety of information sources, including past purchases, preference information provided in profiles or in response to surveys, and the kind of website behavior data that is collected in log files. The engine develops recommendations by looking at the purchases being made by the others in the group and then suggesting them to the individual customer. Different recommendation engine products develop the group identities in different ways; when shopping for a product, you should be sure to get some sense of how accurate the recommendations are, given the characteristics of the customer population you are serving.

The second approach, which we called *market segmentation,* looks at groupings of customers in the external market without reference to what they do on your site. Given such a set of external groupings, you associate each of your customers with the appropriate external group. Such associations can be useful for cross-selling and up-selling insofar as the group membership suggests other products that the customer might like to buy. The external associations, when combined with an internal analysis that shows to which groups most of your customers belong, can also be useful in directing advertising expenditures. For web businesses serving a general consumer population, this kind of market segmentation work can usefully be very sophisticated, employing psychographic factors regarding customer motivation. In business-to-business settings, the external market segmentation might simply depend on enumerating the vertical markets that you serve and looking at the company size of the buyer.

The third approach, which we called *customer segmentation,* looks at groupings *within* the set of customers that you serve. Customer segmentation is almost always a valuable activity. The reason is that, for any business, there are customers who do a lot of business with you and customers who buy only occasionally. If you can find that the most valuable customers fall into an identifiable group that is tied together by something other than their buying habits, it is then much easier to figure out how to find more customers like the valuable ones that you already have. Log file data, purchase data, and customer preference data are all inputs into this process of characterizing the really good customers. Although it is often possible to do some of this characterization work manually, just by looking at frequency counts and other summaries of the data, there are also software tools available to automate this process. These tools can sometimes help you see relationships and dimensions of the customer population that would be invisible in a less sophisticated analysis.

The three approaches are not mutually exclusive but can often be combined with one another in useful ways. The key to creating workable combinations is focusing on what each approach does and then on determining whether it makes a significant contribution in your business. For example, recommendation engines can be very useful at generating cross-selling when buying depends on preferences since group membership is, in fact, a good predictor of preference. But, when buying is driven by external factors, such as form, fit, and function of equipment, group membership is not a good predictor for cross-selling opportunities, and recommendation engines are consequently less useful.

For virtually any web business, including even businesses that sell a single product, working with groupings of customers, in addition to working with customers as individuals, is an important part of engaging your customers effectively. Understanding the groups that you serve is a critical part of understanding your company's position in the market. Knowing where you and your customers stand in the big picture is essential to being effective and to the point in relating to them personally.

Key Ideas

- Understanding your customers as members of groups is an essential part of engaging them as individuals. The group identity provides a context for identifying customer needs and preferences. It makes one-to-one engagement more efficient and is often the basis for cross-selling and up-selling.

- There are different tools and approaches for identifying groups of customers and for putting the group identities to use. The approaches can often be combined. Selecting the right combination depends on understanding what the approaches do and how they connect with the particulars of your business.
- One approach, depending on software tools known as recommendation engines, works well if customer preference, as opposed to external need, is an important component of the purchase process. Recommendation engines automatically use group preferences, with groups formed from within your customer population, to make recommendations to individuals. Their focus is on providing automated interaction with the customer. They may be relatively ineffective in providing useful insights for marketers.
- Market segmentation is another approach to grouping your customers. It depends on group definitions that come from outside your customer population. The value of the approach is in its ability to connect your customers to the larger market. Such connection—for example, to a particular vertical market—can be an important part of identifying customer needs. It can also help in knowing where to look to find more customers.
- Customer segmentation, unlike market segmentation, looks inside your customer base for groupings. In this regard, customer segmentation is like recommendation engines. It differs from recommendations engines in that the focus is explicitly on defining the customer groups in a way that provides insight for the marketer. It is particularly valuable for identifying the characteristics of your most valuable customers.
- Most businesses can usefully deploy a combination of these approaches.

References in This Chapter

1. Personify's site at **http://www.personify.com/** provides a succinct overview of the Personify Essentials product.
2. *Financial Services Online: Forecasts and Strategies for Acquisition, Retention, and Wallet Share* (Jupiter Communications, New York, 1999), p. 43.
3. Information and white papers about the NetPerceptions approach to building recommendation engines is available at **http://www.netperceptions.com/**.
4. Information about Andromedia's LikeMinds recommendation engine is available on the web at **http://www.andromedia.com/products/likeminds/index.html**.

5. Information about SRI's VALS psychographic segmentation, along with a sample VALS survey, is available at **http://future.sri.com/VALS/VALSindex. shtml**.

Further Reading

An article by Malcolm Gladwell titled "The Science of the Sleeper," appearing in the October 4, 1999, issue of *The New Yorker*, provides an interesting and even hopeful analysis of the potential impact of recommendation engines on the market for books. Gladwell argues that the advent of book superstores over the last decade has favored sales of blockbuster books by well-known authors in part because there is no one in such stores who can make good recommendations about little-known books that you will really like. The collaborative filtering process in recommendation engines might change that, increasing the share of book sales by "sleepers," books by little-known authors that sell well. The article contains a useful description of the way recommendation engines work. More important, it contains some interesting thinking about their impact that goes well beyond the details of web business.

CHAPTER ELEVEN

Building Personalized Engagement

Objectives of This Chapter

- Building on the concepts and approaches introduced in the previous chapters, show how to assemble the pieces required to support personalized customer engagement.
- Identify the three key components of a personalization system, and show what is involved in developing these components.
- Show how you can approach the development of personalized engagement in stages, getting value from each stage while at the same time spreading your investment and learning over time.

Assembling the Pieces

We have come a long way since our initial look at log files. We have moved from using website data as the means to *understand your business* as a whole to using the data to *connect with individual customers.* We looked at different ways to create such customer connections. We explored ways to engage the customer in the personalization process. Then we examined techniques for working with customers as members of groups. We saw that you can connect individuals to the needs and preferences of a group, and we saw that you can connect the groups to the larger market.

If customer engagement were a kit, we would want to sort all these pieces, setting them out neatly on top of a table.

We would then need assembly instructions. The sorting and assembly instructions are the focus of this chapter.

Let's start by stepping back from the details to look at the overall picture of what we are building. As Figure 11–1 shows, the personalization process is actually pretty simple, at least at a conceptual level. It involves connecting the content on your site to information about a customer through some kind of set of rules. The rules themselves, which could be explicitly stated or implicit in the operation of a process such as a recommendation engine, are shaped by your business objectives and your model of the market. Once you have made the connection between a customer and the right content, you need a way to deliver the content.

The valuable insight from this general picture is that you need three *processes* and three *sources of information* to support personalized engagement. The three processes are

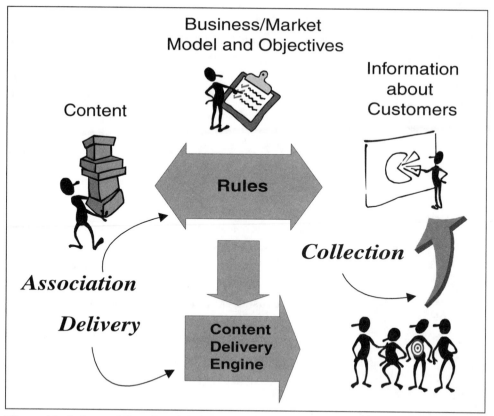

Figure 11–1 Assembling the pieces of personalized engagement

1. **Collection.** You need to get information about your customers.
2. **Association.** You need to connect the information about a particular customer to particular content.
3. **Delivery.** You need to get the content to the customer.

The three sources of information to feed these processes are the *content* itself, the *business model and objectives,* and the *customer data.* Let's look briefly at each of the processes and each of the information sources. Then we can turn our attention to the sequence for putting these pieces together.

The Processes

The processes behind customer engagement have been the focus of the last few chapters. So all we need to do here is pull that information together into the bigger picture of the overall customer engagement effort.

Collection

Collection has been the primary focus of the preceding chapters: How do you get the information that you need? We have looked at the following collection tools and approaches:

- **Web activity.** Log files and other tools for collecting "click stream" data about where visitors come from and what they do on the site are fundamental sources of data.
- **Other observed information.** Regular customers who wish personalized attention can be expected to register on your site. The registration, coupled with cookies, provides you with a way to connect web activity with other activities, such as purchases. This information about individual customer activities is a critically important input into your efforts to connect with and serve the customer. On business-to-consumer sites, it is typically the basis for inferences about customer preferences.
- **Direct preference and profile data.** The simplest way to find out about what a customer wants and needs is to ask. If there is real value for the customer in the engagement, the customer will typically tell you about preferences, content focus, and other needs. In a business-to-business setting, such direct expressions of needs are usually the central core of information you will use for customer engagement, using web activity and purchase information to fill out the picture.

- **External market information.** In some businesses, it makes a great deal of sense to look at customers as members of groups. The groupings can be finely shaded, as with the associations created by a recommendation engine using collaborative filtering. They can also be much coarser, as when looking at trends and requirements for a particular vertical segment—for example, new electronics gear for blue-water fishing vessels. In each case, you are collecting information about your customer's position in a market. The processes supporting such market collection include using subject matter experts, acquiring and analyzing market segment information, and using automated processes such as the ones embedded in collaborative filtering.

Association

Once you have collected information about your customers, you need to then associate that information with the right content or product for each customer as he or she comes to the site. There are two ways to approach this:

1. **Statistically.** You compute the most likely preferences for the customer. Recommendation engines using collaborative filtering are an example of probabilistic association.
2. **By rule.** You select the right content or approach for a customer on the basis of automated logic operating on what you know about the customer (e.g., "If the customer's profile says that he or she is willing to receive e-mail about special offers and if he or she has just purchased a laptop with only 32 megabytes of memory, then send the customer an e-mail with a special offer on a 64-megabyte memory upgrade").

In practice, these two approaches can often be used together. Collaborative filtering is used to recommend products, and a rules-based system drives overall site operation and content selection based on profile information.

Figure 11–1 shows that the inputs to the association process not only require customer information and content but also include the business objectives and the market model. The business model input to the process is not direct and immediate, as in the case of a particular rules lookup. Instead, it gives shape to the overall process, providing answers to questions about what you are trying to achieve through the overall personalization process. Recall the Wine.com example developed in Chapter 10. That company used a rule-based association to connect customers within certain segments to promotional content on Italian wines. The reason for creating such associations in the first place was that Wine.com had determined that sales of Italian wines were smaller than they should be. The business objective, increasing the volume of Italian wine sales, drove the construction of the associations between customers and content.

Delivery

Once you have made the association between a particular customer and the content that you want to present to that customer, you need a way to deliver it. In Chapter 9 we took a detailed look at the options available to you for dynamic delivery of content that is responsive to the needs of individual visitors. Briefly summarized, the range of alternatives includes

- Delivering entire static pages to customers, using different pages for different kinds of customers.
- Using server-side scripting to customize the pages for different visitors. As a simple example, server-side scripts could modify the pages to provide different content for registered visitors than for ones who have not registered.
- Fully dynamic pages that are literally assembled on the fly from a script in response to rules and other associations between the customer and the content.

As noted in the earlier discussion, a number of vendors are offering products to assist in developing fully dynamic content delivery.

The Information Sources

Up to this point in our consideration of the "customer engagement kit," we have been focusing only on the *processes* identified in Figure 11–1: *collection, association,* and *delivery.* Most companies embarking on a program to strengthen their engagement with customers usually do a good job of putting these processes in place. They are the most visible part of the task, and there are ready-made products to help with each key process.

Where most companies run into difficulty is in the organization of the raw materials that feed these processes—that is, the actual information sources that must be managed in order to support personalized customer engagement. As Figure 11–1 shows, there are three sources of information that feed the personalization processes:

1. **Customers.** This source includes information about customers as individuals (needs and preferences) and as groups (segmentation, group trends, and group preferences).
2. **Business.** This source involves business objectives growing from a market model, informed by a realistic picture of how your web business is valued by visitors.
3. **Content.** This source is the content that is to be delivered.

We have talked at length about each of these kinds of information over the course of the preceding chapters. Lets quickly review what we know about them.

Customer Information

Throughout this book, we have looked at a number of different kinds of customer information. The list includes

- Website activity as recorded in log files and similar records
- Registration and other identifying information
- Purchase information
- Information about ads and other content that has already been delivered to the customer, coupled with the customer's response
- Preferences as expressed through profiles and other direct information provided by the customer
- Segmentation information associating the customers with others to form groups

Cookies and the use of identification keys provide the mechanism for tying all of this customer information together. The challenge is organizing the information so that it can be accessed in real time and can thus direct customer interaction. This isn't easy on a busy site. It is one thing to expect customers to wait when they have asked to see their purchase history. It is another when you are trying to access customer information that you want to use to dynamically build a personal home page. Waiting a few seconds as the purchase history report is assembled is acceptable; a slow personal home page is not.

The solution here is to keep options simple when building a dynamic page. For example, the personalized home pages that National Semiconductor delivers are built from an assortment of ready-made product news bulletins. The personalization consists of picking the right bulletins for each particular customer. If you can encode the necessary preference information in the user's cookie, avoiding a database lookup before building the personalized page, things go even faster.

Business Information

In the early chapters of this book, we looked at the use of website activity data to answer fundamental questions about your business: What kinds of customers are coming to your site? What are they using it for?

Think back to the situation faced by the management at CPS, the software company we looked at in Chapter 1 of this book. CPS had a plan for its web business consisting of using free software to create crossover sales of its publishing software and services. The problem, as was discovered through analysis of traffic patterns captured in log file data, was that the typical visitor had no interest in CPS's core products and services. Moreover, as developers, these visitors very probably did not see buying such products and services as part of their job. They were coming to the CPS site because, in their minds, CPS was a source of free tools. In such a circumstance, personalization of home pages and other efforts to engage the customer would very probably fail to produce the desired crossover to product sales. The site's visitors were simply the wrong potential market for what CPS had to sell.

Simply stated, you are going to the trouble to connect customers with content in order to achieve some purpose or set of goals. In CPS's case, the purpose would have been sales of core product; in the case of National Semiconductor, the purpose is to make the site the preferred source for hardware samples; Wine.com wanted to sell more Italian wines; in your case, it is yet something else. You need to be able to identify that purpose: Write it down. You are not pursuing customer engagement as a general good; you are trying to build your business in some way.

Having identified the reasons for investing in customer engagement, you need to be sure that your goals make sense in terms of the visitor population coming to your site. This goes back to the basic requirement to be able to engage the customer in personalization: If personalization does not benefit the customer, he or she won't use it. This would have been the problem at CPS had the company engaged in personalized delivery of information about its products and services. The customers coming to the site, as it turned out, were only interested in free software. Personalized delivery of information that they didn't care about would have been a waste of time and money. The kinds of website data collection and inquiry that we examined in the early chapters of this book provide the framework for avoiding such mistakes by evaluating the matchup between your customers, your content, and your business objectives.

Content Information

You have organized your customer information so that you know what a customer needs and cares about as he or she comes to your website. You have verified that the objectives of the personalization effort are consistent and realistic in terms of your web business. You now need to find the right content for that customer. The process of categorizing and organizing the content on a site to support personalized delivery is a large effort, involving more expense than most companies anticipate.

Looking at a specific example will help illustrate what is involved. We talked earlier about the business-to-business personalization opportunities on the Equilinx site, used by marine engineers as they find replacement parts for ships. Suppose that a customer coming to the site is requesting quotes for the parts and services associated with a diesel engine overhaul. Accessing data about that customer and the particular ship that is being serviced, Equilinx notes that the ship is fitted with an old separator. Separators are essentially a specialized centrifuge that takes oil, diesel fuel, and sludge out of oily water produced during operation of the engine. After separation, the purified water can be returned to the ocean. Because of increasingly strict environmental regulations, there have been significant advances in separator technology over the past few years, including real-time software and radio communications to monitor separator operation and to make automatic adjustments.

Equilinx's business objective is to provide engineering assistance and equipment sourcing over the Internet, binding customers to the site because it saves them time in finding and selecting equipment. From its rule base for guiding customer response, Equilinx knows that a diesel engine overhaul is an opportune time to overhaul or replace the separator. From the customer data, it knows not only that this ship is fitted with an older separator but also that this buyer's profile says that he or she wants to receive engineering recommendations and tips during the selection process.

There are several kinds of information that could be helpful to this customer, beyond the simple suggestion that this is a good time to evaluate the operation and the maintenance of the separator. Equilinx might usefully provide the customer with a list of recent industry trade magazine articles about advances in separator technology, along with links to the actual articles. Equilinx could provide a fact sheet and set of engineering practice recommendations related to separators. New product announcements and news releases from separator manufacturers could be useful. If the customer is interested in looking at new separators, Equilinx would, of course, need to provide product information and sources of supply.

How should Equilinx go about organizing all of this information about separators so that it can present it to the customer quickly, during the equipment sourcing process? After all, the customer's original purpose in coming to the site is locating the parts for an engine overhaul. Consequently, he or she is not going to go through a lot of bother to consider separators. In order for this information to be of real interest to the customer, it must be well organized and easy to use. Clearly, asking the customer to do a full-text search on "separator" and then returning a mixed set of articles, product information, and whatever else the search returns will not suffice. Instead, once Equilinx has used its customer data and rules to decide to present the customer with separator information, it must also then have an orderly, engaging way to do so.

The content about separators needs to be classified in at least a couple of different ways. There needs to be a subject classification so that Equilinx can quickly access information about separators. There also needs to be some kind of usage or application classification so that the Equilinx system can differentiate between general articles about separators, product announcements, engineering guidelines, and product literature. There could also be information coming in from discussion groups on the site, containing comments and experiences by other marine engineers with particular separator models, applications, and service problems.

This information not only must be classified according to subject matter and use but also must be sequenced. What should Equilinx present to the customer first? What is the best way to explain why this distraction from the original purpose of finding engine overhaul parts is worth the customer's time and attention? Then what is the best way to quickly provide a busy, harried buyer with an overview of what is new and important in separator technology?

The point of going into such detail with a specific example is to show you why the process of organizing and classifying your content takes a significant investment of time, money, and experience. The experience is, in some ways, the ingredient that is hardest to come by. You need to organize your content, deliver it to interested customers, and then learn from those customers about what works and what doesn't. It is hard to get it all right the first time. The need to improve the organization and usability of your content, stepwise, is one of the principal reasons to approach customer engagement through a staged development effort.

A Staged Development Plan

A company's approach to customer engagement and personalization on its website is always changing, if only because the business objectives keep changing. For example, after Wine.com's campaign to increase customer attention to Italian wines had its desired effect, the company was free to focus its personalization efforts elsewhere. The pace of change is particularly fast when a company is first setting up the processes and background information required to support personalization. There is much to do, and it can't all be done at once. The problem is finding an orderly way to proceed that, from the outset, provides valuable business results for the company and real utility for the customer.

There is, of course, no single, "right" script for staging the development of customer engagement for all companies, but there are some fundamentals. We know, for example, that you need to develop the quality and organization of your content, the sophistication of your business objectives, and the depth of knowledge of your customers and that you need to move these three things forward simultaneously. Sophisticated business objectives and weak, poorly structured content won't succeed, nor will great content and sketchy knowledge of your customers.

The development process of creating better organized content, deeper knowledge of customers, and more sophisticated business objectives is almost certainly continuous, proceeding in many small steps, month after month. Even so, however, it is useful to draw some demarcation lines through the process to break it into stages. Identifying specific stages helps define the direction and objectives of the development. Working from the different kinds of basic information that you need about customers, it is useful to think in terms of three stages:

1. The first stage involves *engaging the individual customer.*
2. The second stage involves *engaging customers in the context of groups.*
3. The third stage involves *growing the engagement over time.*

We will look at the kinds of content organization, customer information, and business insight required for each of these stages. As you will see, the stages build on one another in an orderly way. If you are currently developing customer engagement on your website, it should be possible to create a plan that assigns definite dates for the transitions from stage to stage for your company.

Engaging the Individual Customer

The goal of this first stage is to begin collecting information about your customers as individual people or companies and to provide them with personalized service. In short, the goal is to begin the engagement.

Upon entering this stage, you very probably have an operating website that delivers the same content, in the same way, to every visitor. If it is an e-commerce site, every customer does business with you in the same way. At the end of this stage, you will have built up the following information and capabilities:

- **Customer information.** You will have profile, preference, and purchasing information about your regular, registered customers.
- **Business information.** You will have identified the key benefits to your business and to your customers that are to be obtained from personalized engagement.
- **Content information.** Your site content will be classified and organized in a way that enables you to easily deliver news and information about specific products, services, and interest areas on the basis of visitor profiles.

In a sense, your focus during this first stage is on figuring out how to set up a trade of information and service with your customers. What information about their needs and preferences would be valuable to you? In other words, what do you want out of the trade? What will you be able to give them in return to make them want to tell you about themselves? What is the business benefit to both of you? Approaching this stage in terms of this kind of trade is useful because it gets you thinking about your *objectives* rather than about the *mechanisms* of personalization. Focusing on the *reasons* for engaging your customers rather than on *how* you engage them is the right mind-set for this stage.

If your customers complete purchases on the web, dealing with the mechanics of the purchase process is a good place to start with simple one-to-one engagement. It also provides a good example of the kind of simple trading off of mutual benefits that characterizes this first stage. You are interested in completing the sale as quickly as possible, removing all impediments to converting the visitor from a looker into a buyer. Once the customer is ready to buy, he or she shares that same objective. If the path from selection to sale is blocked with a lot of forms that have to be filled out, the likelihood of the customer's not completing the sale increases.

So you and your customer have the basis for a trade. If the customer provides you with purchase order, billing, and other information necessary to complete the deal, each subsequent sale is easier for both of you.

The same kind of trading logic, focused on swapping information for better service and performance, continues to apply as the personalization becomes more sophisticated. As National Semiconductor found, customers will provide you with information about the problems that they are working on if you make it easier for them to find out what they need to solve the problems. Equilinx is betting that customers will share inventory information if that makes finding replacements quicker and cheaper.

At the end of this stage, you should have rich profile and requirement information from each of your important customers so that you can more effectively meet their needs. You should also know which of those kinds of interactions are most important for your business, and you should have the mechanisms on the content side to get each customer the information that he or she needs.

Engaging Customers in the Context of Groups

The first stage lays the foundation for thinking about your customers as members of groups: You know something about their needs and so can begin to look for patterns in those needs. The outcomes from the second stage are as follows:

- **Customer information.** You will have found useful ways to organize your customers into groups that enable you to better anticipate their needs and interests.
- **Business information.** You will have identified the cross-selling and up-selling opportunities that are most attractive for your businesss and will have developed mechanisms to drive the cross-selling and up-selling.
- **Content information.** Organization of your content will have become more sophisticated to reflect the finer granularity of interest by different customer segments and the richer connections between related products or services.

If the first stage is characterized by *finding out* what the customer wants and then delivering it, this second stage is all about *anticipating* what the customer wants that he or she has not told you about. As we noted in our exploration of the use of customer groupings in Chapter 10, these "wants" can be driven by preference or by logical requirements. *Preferences* tend to be more important in consumer applications where you might, for example, suggest a book that the buyer might enjoy. *Requirements* tend to be more important in business-to-business settings;

for example, knowing what kinds of oil and water separators are currently finding most application for tanker slop water is very probably important information to the group of customers who are tanker operators.

The distinction between preferences and requirements leads to a separation in the approaches followed by different web businesses in this second stage of customer engagement. In business-to-consumer operations, where preference can matter a great deal, recommendation engines using collaborative filtering are often an important part of the second stage. In business-to-business operations, where standard industry practice and requirements are relatively more important, formation of groups is more likely to be on the basis of well-defined criteria, and cross-selling is more likely to be driven from explicit rules.

The notion of making a trade with the customer is still present during this stage. Cross-selling works only when it benefits the customer as well as the seller. But the trade is less explicit than during the first stage, where you are making a direct request to the customer for information that must, correspondingly, provide the customer with direct benefit. During this second stage, the segmentation or recommendation information requires less direct customer input. This makes the trading subtler and, sometimes, more risky: There is a higher probability of alienating buyers when you are providing cross-sell and up-sell information that they did not request directly.

Growing the Engagement over Time

The term *customer engagement* can be understood in a number of different time frames. At one extreme, you want to engage the customer while he or she is visiting your site. At the other, you want to engage the customer over a course of years, growing and extending the relationship. In building a system to support customer engagement, the necessary, very early stages of the development focus on the short-term engagement. As your approach to engagement matures, you can begin to manage the relationship with a longer view and broader objectives. The third stage of our development plan begins to address the issue of engaging the customer in different ways throughout the customer life cycle.

The principles at work here are not at all unique to web businesses. In fact, it is during this stage that you want, if possible, to stop connecting with your customers *only* as a web business, opening up multiple channels of communication including face-to-face contact, telephone, and e-mail. Good customers whom you work with over time trust you with more information and are more likely to rely on the recommendations that you make. Engineers working from the

National Semiconductor site over time are more likely to use design tools that National provides. Port engineers who have purchased from Equilinx over a period of years will be more likely to turn to Equilinx for technical information about new products.

Here are the kinds of developments that will be associated with this stage:

- **Customer information.** You will keep track of information over time, of course. More importantly, you will collect *different kinds* of information as the engagement moves forward.
- **Business information.** You will have a clear picture of the customer life cycle and of how to maximize the benefit of the engagement—for both you and the customer—at each stage of the life cycle. You will know which parts of the life cycle are most profitable. You will be able to focus operations on moving customers to that life cycle stage and on extending the life of that stage.
- **Content information.** Content will be separated and organized by life cycle stage as well as by other kinds of segmentation. Content will be delivered across different channels, not just the web.

The National Semiconductor experience provides a concrete example of these ideas in action. National has learned to recognize the stages of a development life cycle as a customer moves a new product from early design, through prototyping and testing, and then into production. As a customer moves from stage to stage, National provides different services, through different channels. In the final stages, the relationship relies heavily on face-to-face interaction, with a National Semiconductor account manager working directly with the customer to coordinate component supply during production.

Stages, Summarized

As you can see, the three development stages build on one another in terms of the information that you gather, your understanding of the business, and the infrastructure required to deliver the personalized engagement. You begin by collecting information about individual customers, articulating the general goals of the customer engagement, and organizing content in a way that enables delivery in response to profile preferences. You move forward to understanding how your customers fit together into distinct groups with distinct needs and preferences, defining cross-selling and up-selling objectives, and organizing your content in a more fine-grained way to facilitate such cross-selling. Eventually, you reach the point where you understand how your customer relationships change over time.

You have a model of how to fit those changes in with your business goals and to support sophisticated organization of your content so that you deliver appropriate information for different kinds of customers at different life cycle stages, across different channels. Figure 11–2 summarizes this progression from stage to stage.

Summary

Web customer engagement means providing each customer with the content that he or she needs in a way that furthers your business objectives. There are three parts to that formula: *customers, content,* and *business objectives.* Developing a successful web customer engagement program requires paying attention to all three parts.

The actual mechanisms for extending and connecting these three essential components comprise another triad: *collection, association,* and *delivery.* You collect information about your customers and about how they view your business, using log file data, profile data, purchase information, and other resources. You then use this customer information, combined with an understanding of what

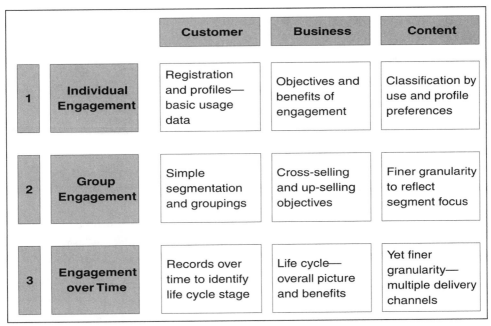

		Customer	Business	Content
1	Individual Engagement	Registration and profiles— basic usage data	Objectives and benefits of engagement	Classification by use and profile preferences
2	Group Engagement	Simple segmentation and groupings	Cross-selling and up-selling objectives	Finer granularity to reflect segment focus
3	Engagement over Time	Records over time to identify life cycle stage	Life cycle— overall picture and benefits	Yet finer granularity— multiple delivery channels

Figure 11–2 Staged development for customer engagement

you are trying to accomplish in the way of business objectives, to associate particular customers with particular content. You then deliver the content.

Collection relies on a broad array of techniques and resources, ranging from log file analysis to personal profiles and external demographic information. It comprises most of the techniques that we have discussed in the preceding chapters of this book.

Association can take the form of collaborative filtering and recommendation engines. It can also rely on logic encoded in scripts or in tables of rules, allowing you to connect content with customers on the basis of preference, history, vertical market, or other segment information.

The delivery mechanisms can start out simply, relying just on scripts running on a web server. At the other extreme, there are sophisticated, high-capacity dynamic publishing tools that cache content and assemble pages in real time.

The key development tasks required to build personalized customer engagement revolve around collecting and preparing the key ingredients: the customer information, business objectives, and content. In this chapter, we explored a simple three-stage sequence that enables you to take a stepwise approach to developing these three core ingredients. The first stage focuses on tying individual customers more closely to your business by responding to their direct needs and preferences. The second stage expands the engagement by working with customers within the context of group associations. The third stage recognizes that engagements develop and change over time, so you need to position your company to respond differently to customers as they move forward with you throughout a complete customer engagement life cycle.

Key Ideas

- Customer engagement on the web grows from providing customers with the content that they need in a way that furthers your business objectives.
- To do this, you need mechanisms to collect customer information, associate the right content with the right customer, and to then deliver the content. The collection process consists of the techniques that we have discussed throughout the early chapters of this book. The association uses the individual and group personalization frameworks developed in the middle chapters of this book. The delivery ranges from simple scripting to use of state-of-the-art content management products.

- Success depends on progressive development of the information that you have about your customers, of your understanding of what works for your business, and of the organization of your content.
- It is possible to frame up this progressive development effort in a series of stages, progressing from meeting the needs of the individual customer, to responding to the customer as a member of a number of groups, to responding to the customer in different ways over time.

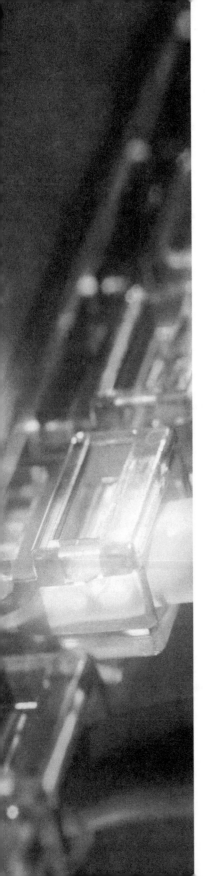

Index

Addison-Wesley Professional

How to Register Your Book

Register this Book
Visit: **http://www.aw.com/cseng/register**
Enter the ISBN*
Then you will receive:

- Notices and reminders about upcoming author appearances, tradeshows, and online chats with special guests
- Advanced notice of forthcoming editions of your book
- Book recommendations
- Notification about special contests and promotions throughout the year

*The ISBN can be found on the copyright page of the book

Visit our Web site
http://www.aw.com/cseng
When you think you've read enough, there's always more content for you at Addison-Wesley's web site. Our web site contains a directory of complete product information including:

- Chapters
- Exclusive author interviews
- Links to authors' pages
- Tables of contents
- Source code

You can also discover what tradeshows and conferences Addison-Wesley will be attending, read what others are saying about our titles, and find out where and when you can meet our authors and have them sign your book.

Contact Us via Email
cepubprof@awl.com
Ask general questions about our books.
Sign up for our electronic mailing lists.
Submit corrections for our web site.

cepubeditors@awl.com
Submit a book proposal.
Send errata for a book.

cepubpublicity@awl.com
Request a review copy for a member of the media interested in reviewing new titles.

registration@awl.com
Request information about book registration.

We encourage you to patronize the many fine retailers who stock Addison-Wesley titles. Visit our online directory to find stores near you.

Addison-Wesley Professional
One Jacob Way, Reading, Massachusetts 01867 USA
TEL 781-944-3700 • FAX 781-942-3076